Rachel
Carson

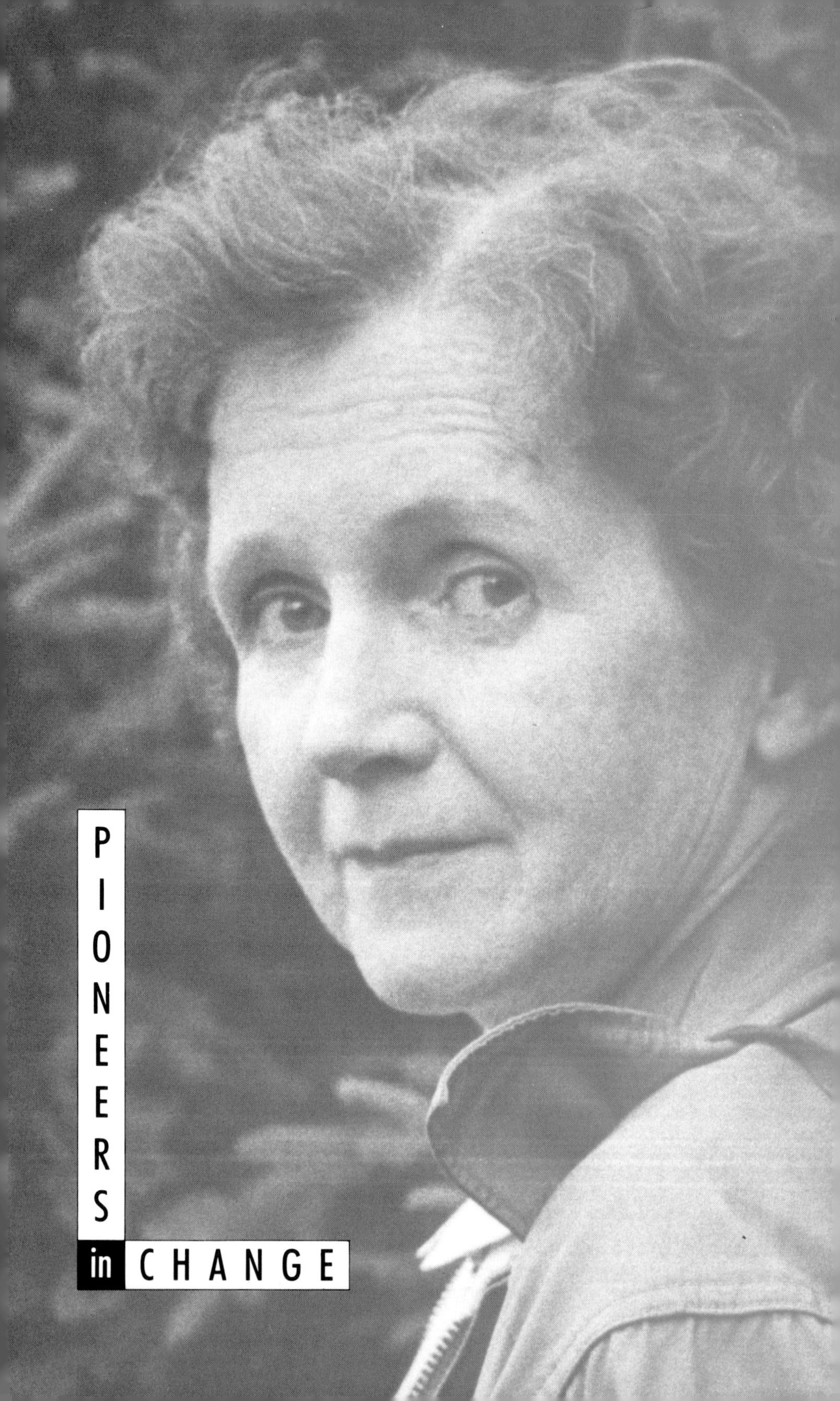
PIONEERS
in CHANGE

Rachel Carson

LESLIE A. WHEELER

Silver Burdett Press

For my niece, Claudia Wheeler Rappe, who loves nature, knows it's wrong to "kill" it, and tries not to.

CONSULTANTS:

Robert M. Goldberg
Consultant to the Social Studies Department
(formerly Department Chair)
Oceanside Middle School
Oceanside, New York

Karen E. Markoe
Professor of History
Maritime College of the State
University of New York

TEXT CREDITS:
Text credits are listed on page 137.

PHOTOGRAPH ACKNOWLEDGMENTS:
Animals Animals: p. 96; AP/Wide World Photos: p. 115; The Beinecke Rare Book and Manuscript Library, Yale University: pp. 4, 8, 21, 29; Bettmann Archive: p. 94; The Ferdinand Hamburger Jr. Archives of the Johns Hopkins University: p. 34; Rachel Carson Council, Inc.: pp. ii and 100 (photo by Erich Hartmann), 6, 10, 57 (photo by Shirley Briggs), 73 (photo by Edwin Gray), 84 (photo by Shirley Briggs), 123.

SERIES AND COVER DESIGN:
R STUDIO T • Raúl Rodríguez and Rebecca Tachna.

PHOTO RESEARCH:
Omni-Photo Communications, Inc.

Published by Silver Burdett Press, Inc., a division of
Simon & Schuster, Inc., Englewood Cliffs, NJ 07632

Library of Congress Cataloging-in-Publication Data

Wheeler, Leslie.
Rachel Carson / Leslie A. Wheeler.
p. cm.—(Pioneers in change)
Includes bibliographical references and index.
Summary: Describes the life and work of the biologist and
conservationist, examining the role of her writing in initiating
the environmental movement.
1. Carson, Rachel, 1907–1964—Juvenile literature. 2. Ecologists—
United States—Biography—Juvenile literature.
[1. Carson, Rachel, 1907–1964. 2. Conservationists. 3. Biologists.]
I. Title. II. Series. QH31.C33W44 1991
574'.092—dc20
[B]   90-26585
[92]   CIP
                                             AC

Manufactured in the United States of America.
ISBN 0-382-24167-3 [lib. ed.]
10 9 8 7 6 5 4 3 2 1
ISBN 0-382-24174-6 [pbk.]
10 9 8 7 6 5 4 3 2 1

CONTENTS

1

A Seashell to Her Ear

Through her books Rachel Carson changed the way people looked at the sea, then at the entire planet. But this path-breaking biologist and writer never glimpsed salt water until she was a grown woman. Still, the ocean fascinated Rachel from her earliest years. She dreamed of it and read all she could about it. She also listened to the sound of the sea—a slow, hollow hissing that grew louder, then fainter. She could hear this sound when she held to her ear the conch shell her family kept on the mantel of their parlor in Springdale, Pennsylvania.

Springdale was several hundred miles inland from the Atlantic coast. The town occupied a narrow strip of land along a sweeping curve of the Allegheny River in southwestern Pennsylvania. In early times, the valley of the Allegheny had been a region of great natural beauty. The first white settlers who came into the area in the late 1700s found huge forests of locust, hickory, and chestnut trees. Bear, elk, deer, and wildcats lived in these woods. The river teemed with fish, and owls and other birds filled the skies.

By the early 1900s, the area around Springdale no longer boasted great forests nor abundant wildlife. Industry had begun to leave its often ugly mark on the land. There were now coal mines, iron smelters, steel mills, and factories that turned out glass, paint, and aluminum. Springdale itself had a glue factory and a population of about one thousand.

These changes didn't bother most Americans. Mines, mills, and factories meant progress to them. But the fact that forests and wildlife were fast disappearing alarmed a few people. They felt that certain areas with beautiful scenery and unusual natural features ought to be set aside. In 1872, Congress established Yellowstone National Park—the first national park in the world.

In the early 1900s, people who wanted to preserve forests and wildlife became known as conservationists. Conservation is the protection and wise use of natural resources. A government official named Gifford Pinchot first used this term. Pinchot headed the U.S. Forest Service during the administration of President Theodore Roosevelt. Roosevelt himself was an active conservationist. He added many millions of acres to the nation's forest reserves. In 1903, he also established the first federal wildlife refuge, or safe place, at Pelican Island, Florida.

Although they weren't conservationists, Rachel Carson's parents wanted to live in a place where some natural beauty remained. They found unspoiled land near Springdale.

Rachel's mother, Maria McLean Carson, originally came from Cleveland, Ohio. Born in 1869, she was the daughter of a Presbyterian minister. His death at the age of forty when Maria was only eleven meant that she, her fourteen-year-old sister, and her mother had to manage on their own. The family moved to the town of Washington, Pennsylvania. There the two girls attended the Washington Female Seminary, a Presbyterian school. A talented pianist and singer, Maria joined a local musical group. However, a career as a singer or musician was out of the question. So after graduation Maria turned to schoolteaching as both a more respectable and more certain way of making a living.

In 1894, aged twenty-five, Maria McLean met a young man who shared her love of music. Robert Warden Carson's ancestors had come to America from Scotland. He lived in Pittsburgh and came to town with a visiting church singing group.

That June, the couple married. Maria left her job as a schoolteacher, and she and her new husband moved to Springdale. Robert Carson bought sixty-five acres of wooded land on the outskirts of town. He didn't intend to farm this land. Instead, he hoped to prosper by selling off building lots to people moving into the area from Pittsburgh, as he had.

Meanwhile, Robert Carson planted a ten-acre apple orchard and kept a cow, pigs, chickens, rabbits, and a horse. He supported his family by selling insurance and dealing in real estate. A quiet, dignified man, Robert Carson earned the respect of the townspeople.

Like many other married women at this time, Maria Carson didn't try to combine marriage with a career. She devoted herself to keeping house and raising the children.

Born on May 27, 1907, Rachel Louise Carson was the youngest of three. Her sister, Marian, was ten years older; her brother, Robert, eight years older. Rachel's sister and brother helped look after her. But because they were so much older they could hardly be expected to serve as

Maria McLean Carson with her children, Marian (left), Rachel, and Robert.

playmates. When Rachel was a child of six, Marian was already a young woman of sixteen. Marian practiced the latest dance steps and had begun to think about boys. Robert also had interests of his own that were hard to share with his "baby" sister. He liked to tinker with things and at one point built his own crystal-detector radio receiver.

As the youngest child, Rachel formed an especially close bond with her mother. Maria Carson had named Rachel after her own mother. And while Rachel was still quite young, Maria Carson taught her about the things she loved best. One day when mother and daughter were sitting on the back porch, Maria Carson told two-year-old Rachel to listen. Rachel heard a bird singing, and her mother explained that it was a meadowlark.

Maria Carson had a deep respect and love for all living creatures. Even spiders were sacred. Maria Carson put them out of the house, rather than kill them. When her son, Robert, came home with a rabbit he had shot, Maria made no secret of her disapproval. But she did clean and cook the rabbit.

Rachel herself finally asked Robert why he shot rabbits. When he replied that hunting was fun, she said that it couldn't be much fun for the rabbits. She thought it was better to watch the rabbits nibbling on greens and hopping along than to kill them. Robert began to feel ashamed of what he was doing.

Rachel delighted in watching the various animals, tame as well as wild, on the Carson property. When she was four, her mother let her scatter cracked corn for the chickens. She also liked to watch her little dog, Candy, play with the pigs. While a pig was lying down, Candy would climb onto its back.

Rachel spent hours exploring the nearby woods and

Rachel Carson and her dog, Candy.

streams. "I can remember no time when I wasn't interested in the out-of-doors," she later said. "I was a rather solitary child and spent a great deal of time in woods and beside streams, learning [about] the birds and insects and flowers."

When she was six years old, Rachel entered the first grade at the Springdale Grammar School. Although she would have less time to wander in the woods, Rachel was looking forward to school. Already her mother had encouraged her to handle the books in the Carson's parlor library. Rachel would turn the pages and spell out some of the words. Now at school she would learn to read.

In the early years of her schooling, Rachel was often absent for long periods because of illness. At one point, she came down with scarlet fever. In those days before antibiotics—special drugs that cure disease—scarlet fever could be fatal. To prevent her from catching other dangerous childhood diseases like whooping cough and the measles, her mother sometimes kept Rachel at home.

Rachel's schoolwork didn't suffer, however, because her mother tutored her at home. She not only kept up with her classmates, but did better than many who had perfect attendance records.

Without radio or television to entertain them in the evening, the Carsons turned to music and books. Maria Carson played the piano, and the whole family joined in the singing of popular songs like "Carry Me Back to Old Virginy" and "Beautiful Ohio." Or the children listened, spellbound, crunching on apples from the family orchard, while Maria Carson read aloud.

After she had learned to read herself, Rachel particularly delighted in the animal stories written and illustrated by the Englishwoman Beatrix Potter. She also enjoyed *Freckles* by the popular American woman writer Gene Stratton Porter. This was the story of an Irish-American orphan boy who runs away from the orphanage and finds work guarding the valuable timber of the Limberlost Swamp against thieves. In the end, he marries a wealthy young woman and lives happily ever after. Along with the book's adventure and romance, Rachel enjoyed its beautiful nature descriptions.

At the age of ten, Rachel decided she wanted to be a writer herself. A big source of inspiration was *St. Nicholas*, a popular children's magazine of the time. The magazine invited readers to send in original stories and pictures to a special department called The St. Nicholas League. It published the best stories with the authors' names and ages,

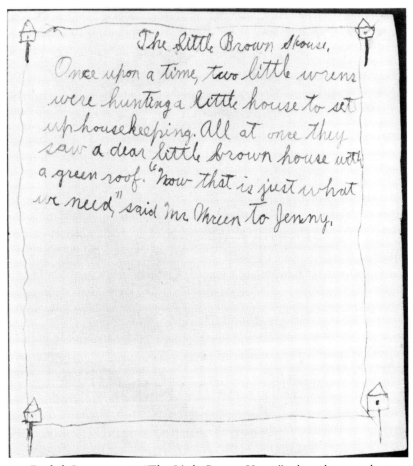

Rachel Carson wrote "The Little Brown House" when she was about seven.

but all contributors became members of the league. A number of these young contributors, including Stephen Vincent Benét, Eudora Welty, and Sterling North, went on to become famous writers.

Rachel didn't doubt she could write as well as any of the *St. Nicholas* authors. Besides, she had an idea for an exciting story. In 1914 World War I had broken out in Europe. At first the United States had tried to stay out of the war. In 1917, however, the nation decided to send troops to fight in Europe. Rachel's brother, Robert, now eighteen, gave up his plans to study electrical engineering in favor of joining the U.S. Army Air Service. He went to Texas to attend training camp. From there he wrote the family about his experiences. One of these Rachel made into a story.

Titled "A Battle in the Clouds," Rachel's story had to do with a famous Canadian aviator. In an air battle with German fliers, the aviator hangs from the wing of his damaged plane to balance it and keep it from crashing. The Germans are so impressed with his courage and daring that they hold their fire until the plane has safely landed. Later, however, the aviator is killed in an accident at the training camp in Texas.

St. Nicholas published "A Battle of the Clouds" in its September 1918 issue. Rachel was thrilled to see her words in print and win a silver badge. She also received a check for ten dollars.

Encouraged by her success, Rachel sent two more stories to *St. Nicholas*. The magazine accepted both. "A Message to the Front" (February 1919) describes the moment when discouraged French soldiers receive word that the United States is joining the fighting on their side. "A Famous Sea-Fight" (August 1919) describes U.S. naval officer George Dewey's famous victory over the Spanish fleet at Manila Bay, the Philippines. Dewey's victory occurred during the Spanish-American War of 1898.

Because of her special abilities and shy manner, Rachel's teachers noticed her more than her classmates in elementary school and later in high school. When Rachel was fourteen, she entered Springdale High School. Minerva Baker, the

9

Rachel, Robert, and Marian Carson during World War I. Robert Carson is in the uniform of the U.S. Army Air Service.

assistant principal, was so impressed with some of Rachel's compositions that she read them aloud at a teachers' meeting.

The location of the Carson home on the outskirts of town made it more difficult for would-be friends to seek Rachel out. Also, she herself didn't make friends easily or lightly. And her mother encouraged her to be somewhat particular. Still, Rachel didn't lack companions her own age.

On Saturdays, Irene Mills often came to spend the day with Rachel. When the weather kept them indoors, the two girls amused themselves with magazines, books, and the piano. Otherwise, they passed the time exploring the Carson property. On Sunday afternoons, another friend, Charlotte Fisher, often stopped at the Carson house for tea, cookies, and apples. Together with Rachel's mother, the girls discussed books they were reading. At the time, Springdale had no public library. But Charlotte made frequent trips to a library in Pittsburgh and brought back books for the Carsons as well as for herself.

A third friend was Mildred Krumpe, one of the eight children of a local dentist. While the other children played their noisy games in the Krumpe backyard, Rachel and Mildred stood on the sidelines. Both were quiet, book-loving, and not particularly athletic. But they joined in eagerly when a group formed around the piano for singing.

When she was sixteen, Rachel parted company with Mildred Krumpe and other friends at Springdale High. Springdale High was only a two-year school. Many of its students completed high school at Peabody High in East Liberty. To get there, they had to take a thirty-five-minute train ride. Rachel, however, decided to go to a school closer to home. Parnassus High in New Kensington was only two miles by streetcar from home.

Rachel did almost as well at Parnassus as she had at Springdale High. Her two-year average at Springdale was 93.7; at Parnassus, it was 93.5. Rachel's studiousness was what impressed her classmates the most about her. As the verse printed in her high school yearbook next to her picture put it:

> Rachel's like the mid-day sun
> Always very bright
> Never stops her studying
> Until she gets it right.

Her high marks meant that Rachel was able to win a college scholarship. Without such financial aid, Rachel might not have been able to go to college. Her father had failed to make a fortune from the sale of building lots. Instead, by selling off the lots one at a time, he made just enough to allow the family to live modestly.

Some of Rachel's high school classmates looked to college as a place to have a good time. Rachel, however, had serious plans. At college, she hoped to realize her girlhood ambition of becoming a writer. As she said good-bye to her family and her beloved woods and streams, she had no idea how her goals were to change in the next four years.

CHAPTER

```
┌─────────┐
│         │
│    2    │
│         │
└─────────┘
```

Writer or Biologist?

In September 1925, Rachel enrolled at Pennsylvania College for Women, later known as Chatham College. The campus was located on a high bluff north and east of the business district of Pittsburgh. Its grassy slopes, wooded knolls, flower beds, and ivy-covered halls contrasted sharply with the smoky factories of the city below.

Besides having an attractive campus, Chatham was only sixteen miles by train from Springdale. Rachel's classmates called Mrs. Carson "the commuter," because she visited the college every other weekend. On alternate weekends, her daughter went home.

Other advantages were the small size of the student body—about three hundred—and the college's high academic standards. Finally, the college offered a few scholarships to help students meet the $1,000-a-year cost of tuition and room and board. Chatham was only able to offer Rachel

$100. However, the college president, Cora Helen Coolidge, and Dean Mary Marks were able to get some of their well-to-do friends to help out, privately and unofficially.

By the end of the fall semester, Rachel had justified Coolidge and Marks's faith in her. She was one of the ten highest-ranking first-year students at the college. Her seriousness about her studies set her apart from many of her classmates.

During the so-called Roaring Twenties, many Americans, especially young people, gave themselves over to having a good time. On college campuses, students wore raccoon coats and took part in pranks like swallowing live goldfish and perching on top of flagpoles. Young women, known as flappers, raised their hemlines above their knees, wore rouge and lipstick, and bobbed their hair—cut it short. Rachel had bobbed hair, but that was the only thing she had in common with the flappers.

Many of the young women who went to Chatham came from wealthier families than Rachel's. They wore expensive "college clothes," had generous allowances to spend, and enjoyed dates, proms, dances, and holidays. Only a few had clear-cut plans for a career.

Nevertheless, Rachel might still have been popular if she had tried to be. Instead, she spent long hours studying and generally went her own way. She was friendly with the other students, but kept her distance. As one classmate put it, "She wasn't anti-social. She just wasn't social."

Rachel did take part in sports, though. She tried out for the class hockey, baseball, and basketball teams. She attended so many practice sessions that she was a frequent substitute, though never a regular member of any of these teams.

Rachel also became a reporter for the semimonthly student paper, *The Arrow*. Before the end of her freshman year, the paper's special literary supplement, *Englicode*, published a long short story of hers. "The Master of the Ship's Light" was noteworthy for its beautiful descriptions of the sea.

Although Rachel had yet to view the ocean, it continued to fascinate her. One night when the wind and rain beat against the window of her college dormitory, a line of poetry came into Rachel's head: "For the mighty wind arises, roaring seaward, and I go." The line was from *Locksley Hall* by the British poet Alfred, Lord Tennyson. It struck a chord deep within Rachel. She felt that somehow her own path led to the sea.

The ocean wasn't Rachel's only subject, however. Other stories revealed her understanding of animals. "Why I Am a Pessimist," for example, is the story of a cat who complains he is both deprived of his independence and ignored in the household where he lives. In "Keeping an Expense Account," on the other hand, Rachel wrote directly about herself and her need, as a scholarship student, to watch every penny.

Still other stories focused on particular choices and conflicts. "The Golden Apple" is Rachel's humorous retelling of a famous Greek myth. Three goddesses ask Paris, a prince of Troy, to decide which of them is to get the golden apple marked for the most beautiful. Juno, the queen of the gods, promises to make Paris the ruler of Europe and Asia if he chooses her. Minerva, the goddess of war and wisdom, promises victory in battle against the Greeks. Venus, the goddess of love, offers Paris Helen, the most beautiful woman in the world. Helen, however, happens to be married to a Greek king. When Paris chooses Venus and then seizes Helen, he sets off a tragic war between the Greeks and the Trojans.

In her version of the myth, Rachel makes it clear that she thinks the goddesses were foolish to let Paris, a mere mortal man, decide among them. She doesn't think much of Paris for his choice either. But through the character of Venus, Rachel lets us know she believes that, like Paris, most men will choose beauty over wisdom and courage.

Another story that reveals a conflict is "Broken Lamps." The hero is an engineer who dreams of building a perfect bridge, combining beauty and strength. His wife, however, seems not to appreciate the importance of his dream. Then her sudden illness teaches him a lesson. The engineer realizes that the beauty and strength he has been seeking in a bridge exist elsewhere. These qualities have been present all along in another human being—his wife.

"Broken Lamps" appeared in the *Englicode* issue of May 27, 1927, the date of Rachel's twentieth birthday. The story won the annual prize offered by Omega, the campus English club. As her sophomore year came to an end, Rachel seemed well on her way to becoming a successful writer. Yet at the same time, she was beginning to rethink her goals.

The science course Rachel took in her sophomore year was responsible for this shift. Since two semesters of science were required for graduation, Rachel enrolled in Biology 1 and 2. Little did she expect how Mary Skinker's teaching would make the subject come alive for her.

Thirty-four-year-old Mary Skinker combined knowledge of biology with an intense enthusiasm for the subject. She did her best to share her excitement with students. Rachel found Mary Skinker's enthusiasm contagious. Under the guidance of this gifted and inspiring teacher, she began to take a different view of biology. Instead of a dull, required course, she saw it as a fascinating science.

As her junior year started, Rachel was beginning to doubt she wanted to continue with English as her major, or special field of study. It wasn't that she was less interested in writing, but rather that she was now more interested in science. One-half of Rachel's third-year program consisted of science courses in such areas as zoology—the science of animals and animal life. In these science courses, she never averaged less than an A minus.

Rachel also continued to shine in the English courses of Professor Grace Croff. Like Mary Skinker, Croff was a first-rate teacher. She predicted a literary career for Rachel, however. At one point, Croff had the class write triolets, eight-line poems with a difficult rhyme scheme. She read samples of the best student poems before the entire class, including this one:

> Butterfly poised on a thistle's down,
> Lend me your wings for a summer's day.
> What care I for a kingly crown,
> Butterfly poised on a thistle's down,
> When I might wear your gossamer gown,
> And sit enthroned on an orchid spray?
> Butterfly poised on a thistle's down,
> Lend me your wings for a summer's day!

Rachel's accomplishment awed her classmates. How did she do it? they asked. Rachel replied that knowing a triolet was supposed to be light, she thought of the lightest things she could—a butterfly and thistledown.

By her junior year, Rachel had found a place for herself at Chatham. She was still somewhat of a loner. But now she belonged to a small group of juniors and seniors with similar interests. Most of her friends were either English majors or students she had met in her science classes. They served on the staffs of *The Arrow, Englicode,* or the college yearbook, *Pennsylvanian.* They were also hockey players.

Rachel was the goalkeeper on the junior class field hockey team. At 115 pounds, she didn't present a great barrier, but opposing players seldom got past her. The entire team did so well that it won the 1927–28 school championship.

After games, Rachel's teammates piled into someone's car for a trip to Reymer's, a popular ice-cream parlor. Rachel was often invited to come along, but she usually refused. It needn't be expensive, a teammate insisted at one point. Rachel could get a lime soda for only fifteen cents, if she wanted. But Rachel shrugged and said, "Who's got fifteen cents?"

Nevertheless, Rachel did join enthusiastically in other activities like a moonlit sledding party in February 1928. According to Rachel, she and the other girls had "a perfectly glorious time" coasting down the hill on two sleds and numerous trays. Afterward, the girls gathered in the parlor of their dormitory before a roaring fire. They feasted on sandwiches, potato salad, and coffee. Then they turned off all the lights and sat in the firelight, singing popular songs till midnight.

Other happy experiences were the field trips—visits for the purpose of firsthand observation—that Mary Skinker took her students on. A classmate noted that on these occasions Rachel's "bobbed hair ruffled in the wind," and "her blue eyes [were] intent and observing."

Skinker took them to locations along the interurban railway between Pittsburgh and Butler, Pennsylvania. This was a region of forests, ponds, and streams enclosed by steeply rising cliffs. The students and their teacher searched for trailing arbutus and other wildflowers. Once an excited Rachel recognized her first ovenbird. The ovenbird is an American song bird that builds a dome-shaped nest (like an oven) on the ground. They also explored Cook State Forest, a 6,000-acre wilderness. At McConnell's Mill, they investigated the line where a glacier of the last Ice Age had stopped. In the soft stone of a hillside, Rachel discovered a fish fossil.

Rachel's growing love of science made her decide to change her major to biology. Naturally, Mary Skinker was delighted. But Grace Croff and the college president, Cora Coolidge, were upset. They felt that as a writer Rachel had a much better chance of success. By this time, a number of American women had won fame and fortune with their books and magazine articles. But prominent women scientists were few and far between. In the 1920s, opportunities for women in science were pretty much limited to high school or college teaching and a very few government jobs. A woman biologist running her own laboratory and doing her own research was practically unheard of.

Despite the dismay her decision caused, Rachel stuck to it. She spent hours in the science laboratory in the tower of Dilworth Hall on campus.

Still, Rachel did take time out for one big date. On a March weekend, she invited Bob Frye, a junior at Westminster College, to the junior prom. In a letter to a friend, Rachel said she had "a glorious time" at the dance. The day after, Bob Frye took Rachel to a basketball game at his school, some fifty miles from Pittsburgh. She saw him at least once more, the following month.

Rachel's senior year, which started in September 1928, was filled to the brim with studies and student activities. She was taking six science courses and wanted especially to do well in order to justify her change of major. Unfortunately, Mary Skinker wasn't there to offer support and encouragement. The teacher was taking a leave of absence to study for an advanced degree at Johns Hopkins University in Baltimore, Maryland. Rachel missed her a great deal, but kept in touch by means of letters.

Outside of class, Rachel served as proofreader for *The Arrow*. She was also elected president of a new science club. Rachel and two friends, Mary Frye and Dorothy Thompson, who were also biology enthusiasts, had helped to found the club. It was called Mu Sigma—M.S. in the Greek alphabet for Mary Skinker.

Hockey games kept Rachel busy as well. For the first time, the best hockey players from each of the four class hockey teams were chosen to form two honorary "all-star" teams. The two teams, called Army and Navy, competed for the college championship. Rachel was the Navy goalkeeper. At one team meeting, the captain suggested the team arrive on the field with its mascot, a goat. The day of the game, Rachel showed up with not just one but two goats—a nanny and its kid.

The game was notable for its animal antics. By running circles around the girl assigned as its keeper, the goat managed to lash the unfortunate young woman to a tree. It even butted one of the cheerleaders. Then in the second quarter a dog seized the ball when it rolled out of bounds. In the midst of much confusion and laughter, Navy won the game, 6–2.

In her senior year, too, Rachel had to deal with pressing financial problems. Her scholarship money had not proved enough to cover all of her expenses at Chatham. By the time she graduated, she would owe the school more than $1,600.

Rachel Carson at Pennsylvania College for Women.

To make it possible for Rachel to complete her final year, she and the college president worked out a special arrangement. Some of the Carson land that remained was held in Rachel's name—that is, she was the legal owner of this land. Her family agreed to let Rachel sign over to the college two of the Springdale lots. The land would serve as a guarantee that she would pay back both her present debt and what she would owe by graduation. If Rachel found a buyer for the lots, she would be able to pay off her debt in a lump sum. Otherwise, she was to start making regular cash payments to the school, beginning October 1, 1930, with 6 percent interest. Once she had paid off the debt, the lots would be hers again.

Rachel was glad to be relieved for the moment of her financial worries. Now she could enjoy the awards and honors that came to her in May of her senior year. When the editors of *The Arrow* put together their annual "Ideal Senior," they used "Rachel's brains." The editors of the *Pennsylvanian* paid tribute to her by putting these lines next to her picture:

> A muse of fire that ascends
> The brightest heavens of invention.

By referring to Carson as a muse, they meant that she was a source of inspiration.

The college itself thought highly enough of Rachel's abilities as a scholar to award her her degree magna cum laude—that is, with great distinction. Johns Hopkins University was impressed by Rachel's record, too. The university granted her a year's scholarship as a graduate, or advanced, student in zoology.

As if all this weren't exciting enough, Chatham College had arranged for Rachel to take part in a summer-study program in marine biology at another institution. Marine biology is the study of the living creatures of the sea. Rachel would be attending a major center for this kind of study, the Marine Biological Laboratory at Woods Hole. Woods Hole is located on the southwestern tip of Cape Cod along the Massachusetts coast. Now, at last, Rachel would be able to satisfy her childhood fascination with the sea.

CHAPTER

$$3$$

Woods Hole and Johns Hopkins

Rachel Carson spent June and most of July in Springdale preparing for Woods Hole later in the summer and Johns Hopkins University in the fall. She hemmed dresses, did chores, read, and roamed her beloved trails on the Carson property. The land was still wooded, though some of it had been cleared, and unpaved streets had been cut through it. The Carsons no longer kept pigs, cows, or horses. They only had a few chickens and a family of cats now.

Toward the end of July, Carson said good-bye to her family and traveled by train to Baltimore. She signed up for classes at Johns Hopkins and met with Dr. R. P. Cowles of the zoology department. Dr. Cowles was to be her academic adviser—that is, he would help her select her program of study at the university. After exploring the campus and the city itself, Carson continued on to Washington, D.C. She spent the night at the apartment of Mary Skinker and her sister. Mary herself was vacationing in Virginia at a mountain resort called Skyland.

The next day Carson joined Skinker. She was delighted to see her teacher again. During the day, they rode horseback and played tennis. Not far from their cabin they had a fine view of the Shenandoah Valley below. They climbed or rode up nearby peaks, which gave them other magnificent views. Evenings they sat by the open fire and talked. At the end of the month, they left Skyland together. Skinker returned to Washington. Carson continued on to New York City.

Carson arrived in the city early in the morning. She spent the day sightseeing. Then late in the afternoon, she boarded the Colonial Line passenger boat that was to take her to New Bedford, Massachusetts. Despite a rainstorm, she stayed on deck to see the Statute of Liberty as the boat made its way through New York Harbor. By evening the weather had cleared. Carson left her stuffy little stateroom and returned to the deck. She breathed deeply of the salt air and reveled in the sense of being out at sea beyond sight of land.

At daybreak Carson transferred to the Woods Hole boat and began the sixteen-mile trip up Buzzards Bay. The water was rough, but she remained on deck anyway. At last the boat entered Great Harbor at the southwestern tip of Cape Cod. Now Carson could see the buildings of the U.S. Bureau of Fisheries and the Marine Biological Laboratory (MBL).

Some of the world's finest scientists worked in these libraries and laboratories. They investigated the geology, geography, physics, chemistry, and biology of the oceans. Aboard research vessels of both the Bureau of Fisheries and the MBL, they scoured the depths of the Atlantic Ocean in search of new knowledge. Some of the scientists Carson knew by reputation from the pages of her college textbooks.

Now she was going to meet these scientists in person.

Carson went immediately to the MBL office to sign up for the summer-study program. She was favorably impressed by the main laboratory building and the library where "they seem to have everything." At the MBL dining hall, she could get three meals a day for seven dollars a week. Mary Frye, her laboratory partner from Chatham, was also at Woods Hole for the summer-study program. The two young women shared a rented room in the home of a widow.

The next six weeks were crammed with both work and play. Carson had arranged to have turtle embryos waiting for her at the laboratory. Embryos are animals in the early stages of their growth. Carson's plan was to study the nerves in the brains of these very young creatures. She had already discussed the project with Dr. Cowles. He thought it might be worth publishing in a scientific journal.

To a friend, however, Carson confided that when she thought of all the work that would have to be done before she could publish anything, it made her "sort of sick." To study the embryos, she had to dissect, or cut them apart piece by piece, under a microscope. This was hard on her eyes. Nevertheless, she was excited about her work and felt she was accomplishing something.

Carson also had a chance to study live sea creatures that until now she had only known from textbook descriptions. She observed these creatures in the aquarium of the U.S. Bureau of Fisheries, in the MBL seawater tanks, and on the beach. Before her fascinated eyes, brightly colored fish swam to and fro, starfish slid along, and sea anemone grabbed food with flowerlike feelers.

For fun, Carson and Mary Frye sunbathed on the beach, played tennis, and swam. On weekends, a group might gather for a beach party.

Carson enjoyed being part of a large scientific community. The MBL was a very serious place. Scientists even had their mail delivered to them at their laboratory tables. Since people from the U.S. Bureau of Fisheries laboratory took their meals at the MBL dining hall, Carson had an opportunity to meet them as well. She couldn't help noticing there were few women in the group. But she decided that these were the people she wanted to work with after she got her master's degree, the next step in a college education after a bachelor's degree.

The weeks at Woods Hole passed quickly. Almost before Carson knew it, it was time to return to Baltimore and find a furnished room to rent. This done, she went to Washington, D.C., to call on Elmer Higgins at the U.S. Bureau of Fisheries. Higgins was head of the bureau's Division of Scientific Inquiry. Carson explained that she would be starting work on her master's degree in zoology the following month. She thought she would like to work in the fishery field and would be grateful for any advice Higgins could give her.

Carson asked a lot of questions. Why was fishery research important? What kind of work was the bureau doing right now? What projects were planned for the future? What kinds of opportunities were there for women scientists in government or elsewhere? Could Higgins suggest courses that might be helpful to her in her future work?

Carson and Higgins talked for nearly an hour. He described the fishery research that was being done and spoke of his own work on the life histories of shore fish of the South Atlantic states. He also discussed the other basic sciences that a biologist specializing in his field ought to be familiar with.

As for opportunities for women, Higgins said that these

were pretty much limited to high school and college teaching or government work. Few jobs in industry or even at museums were open to women. Carson didn't let these discouraging words dampen her enthusiasm. She had her heart set on becoming a marine biologist, and that was that.

Two weeks later, Carson was busy with academic work. Classes, together with laboratory work, took up forty-six hours of the week. Outside of class, Carson spent hours reading and preparing. She was up by seven, had breakfast in the university cafeteria, then went to her first class. At half past five she hurried home to wash her face and change her clothes before returning for evening laboratory work.

Caught up though she was with her studies, Carson could hardly close her eyes to events in the outside world. She began her work at Johns Hopkins early in October 1929. On the 29th of the month, the New York Stock Exchange crashed.

As stock prices dropped to an all-time low, investors suffered huge losses. The entire economy was badly shaken. In the months and years that followed, thousands of factories and businesses closed. Millions lost their jobs, their homes, and their life savings. The Great Depression, as this period of hard times was called, lasted until 1939, when World War II broke out.

Carson already missed her family. And she was tired of living in dormitories and rented rooms. She wanted the family to be together during the difficult period that lay ahead. When she could find the time, she looked for a house to rent in the Baltimore area. Finally she found one on the Old Philadelphia Road at Stemmer's Run. The house was thirteen miles from Baltimore. But there was reliable bus and train service into the city so Carson could easily get to and from Johns Hopkins University. Also, the house was

Rachel Carson in the laboratory at Woods Hole, Massachusetts.

only two miles from Chesapeake Bay. It featured a grove of oak trees, a tennis court, and inside, a large open fireplace.

Many telegrams, special-delivery letters, and long-distance telephone conversations later, Carson persuaded her family to move from Springdale. In January 1930, she and her parents were reunited. Her brother, Robert, remained behind in Pittsburgh because of business obligations. Her sister, Marian, had married when Rachel was in college. She also continued to live elsewhere with her husband.

Carson's next problem was to find a job that would enable her to stay in school. With jobs scarce, this was no easy task. Nevertheless, in June 1930, she got her first paying work as a teaching assistant in the general biology course at the Johns Hopkins Summer School. Her duties included getting the laboratory ready for forty-five students, washing the glassware, and seeing that each table was supplied with all necessary equipment. It was hardly exciting work, but Carson liked her "boss," Grace Libby. Libby, in turn, thought well enough of Carson to hire her for every summer school session through 1936.

The summer over, Carson needed to find another job and also a research project for her master's thesis—the research paper she had to write to get her degree. She got a part-time position as a laboratory assistant to Dr. Raymond Pearl, a well-known geneticist. Geneticists study the way different qualities are passed on from parents to their offspring.

Finding a research project proved much more difficult. Carson's experiments with the embryos of turtles, snakes, and lizards had not been successful. She had even tried to study the early development of squirrels. But the squirrels sent to her by an animal supplier in Texas wouldn't breed. Nor could the supplier send Rachel Carson any replacements because he had lost all his animals in a fire.

At this point, Carson asked Dr. Cowles to suggest another subject. Together they decided she should study the pronephros of the channel catfish. The pronephros is the fish's temporary kidney. It begins to develop two days after the egg has been fertilized. By the sixth day, the catfish has outgrown its egg. Thanks to the pronephros, the catfish is able to live as a free-swimming larva, or early form of fish. As the larva continues to grow, a permanent kidney, the mesonephros, develops. Gradually, the permanent kidney takes over the task of filtering the fish's body fluids and draining off unnecessary or harmful chemicals. Meanwhile, the temporary kidney is developing into the head kidney, so-called because it lies toward the front of the body cavity.

When Carson began her study, biologists weren't sure what the head kidney really was or what its function was. They wondered whether the temporary kidney changed itself into the head kidney or whether it grew by itself while the temporary kidney shriveled away. They also wondered whether the head kidney continued to do some of the filtering work or whether it became a blood-producing center.

Carson didn't expect to settle all these questions. Instead, she proposed to study the day-by-day growth of the pronephros from its beginning in the egg through the eleventh day in the free-swimming larva. This involved many hours of work examining thin slices of catfish egg and then of larva under the microscope. It also meant reading several thousand pages in English, German, French, and Italian about the life functions and activities of the catfish. Then Carson's task was to write a complete and accurate description of what she had learned.

Carson labored on this project throughout her second

year at Johns Hopkins. She studied hundreds of microscopic slides and learned to make drawings with the help of a camera lucida. This camera without film carries the image of what it sees to a sheet of paper. The person using the camera can then trace the image with a pencil. The work went slowly. Carson wished she could be a full-time graduate student. But she couldn't afford to give up her laboratory assistant job.

Early in February 1931, Carson wrote Chatham College that she couldn't send any money to reduce her debt to the college. Her father was still trying to find a buyer for the two lots signed over to the college. Her family also hoped to find other ways of making payments on the debt.

A bright spot in this difficult year was the arrival of Carson's brother, Robert. His business in Pittsburgh wasn't doing well, so he found a job in Baltimore as a radio-repairs estimator. One evening Robert returned home with a present for Rachel: a handsome Persian cat. Rachel and her mother were delighted, as both were fond of cats. When Rachel asked Robert where the cat had come from, he explained it had been given to him as part payment on a twenty-dollar repair job. In the cash-short years of the Great Depression, people often traded one thing for another—in this case, a cat plus fifteen dollars to have a radio fixed. Mitzi, as the cat was called, and the kittens she later bore, were beloved members of the Carson household for many years to come.

In the summer of 1931, Carson went back to work at her teaching assistant job. That fall she applied for a position as a part-time assistant in zoology at the University of Maryland at College Park, thirty-five miles away. In his letter of recommendation, Dr. Cowles described Carson as "a young lady of excellent character. She is pleasing in appearance and capable in everything she does. Her scholarship has been high in her undergraduate studies and also in her graduate work here. . . . The students, both male and female, like and respect her, and Miss Grace Libby. . . speaks very highly of her."

Hired in mid-September, Carson began making the seventy-mile round-trip bus ride from Stemmer's Run to College Park several days a week. The rest of the time she worked at Johns Hopkins on her thesis. In the spring of 1932, she finally finished her paper, titled "The Development of the Pronephros During the Embryonic and Early Larval Life of the Catfish." It comprised 108 pages and sixty camera-lucida drawings, plus eight photomicrographs—photographs of very small objects made with a camera fitted to a microscope.

That June, Carson received her master's degree in marine zoology. She was eager to find work in her field. Unfortunately, this was the worst possible time to be looking for a job. Before the end of 1932, more than 12 million Americans—one in every four workers—were unemployed. Many who had jobs were only working part-time. Carson herself belonged to this latter category. She still had her half-time teaching job at the University of Maryland. But it ended in December 1933. From that time until the late summer of 1935, her only employment as a scientist was at the Johns Hopkins Summer School.

Not surprisingly, Carson still wasn't able to make payments on her debt to Chatham College. She finally wrote the college that it was free to sell her Springdale land.

Along with millions of other Americans, Carson and her family hoped and prayed for good times to return. They took heart when Franklin D. Roosevelt was inaugurated president on March 4, 1933. Roosevelt promised Americans

Twenty-six-year-old Rachel Carson at Johns Hopkins University. In 1932, she earned a master's degree in marine biology.

a New Deal. He launched many projects designed to provide jobs for the unemployed. A number of these projects were in the area of conservation. Workers in the Civilian Conservation Corps (CCC) planted trees and fought forest fires. They also cleared paths in national parks and forests and built dams to prevent floods. Many people came to view conservation as exciting and important work.

The Carsons, meanwhile, got by as best they could. They were better off than many. Then on July 6, 1935, tragedy struck. Rachel was working at her laboratory job at Johns Hopkins when the telephone rang. It was her mother calling with sad news. Robert Carson, Senior, had died suddenly.

CHAPTER

4

"Seven-Minute Fish Tales"

When Rachel Carson walked into Elmer Higgins's office at the Bureau of Fisheries, she had no idea she had come to the right place at the right time. But it turned out to be true.

Higgins remembered Carson from her earlier visit, when she was just starting her graduate work at Johns Hopkins. What could he do for her now? Higgins asked. Carson explained that her father had recently died and that she needed another job in addition to part-time teaching. Did Higgins have a position for which she might qualify?

The directness of Carson's approach impressed Higgins. After considering her question for a moment, he asked if she could write. She had done very well in English, Carson said, and had planned to major in the subject before switching to biology.

This was just what Higgins wanted to hear. He happened to be looking for someone who was both a good writer and a biologist. Higgins's boss had decided that the Bureau of Fisheries would prepare fifty-two radio broadcasts about fishery and marine life. Before the invention of television, radio was the best way of reaching a wide audience. The first radio station had gone on the air in 1920. Now, fifteen years later, three out of four American families owned radios. So it made sense for the Bureau of Fisheries to turn to radio. The only difficulty was how to put together a successful series of broadcasts.

Higgins was responsible for the writing and planning of the series. He and his staff jokingly referred to the broadcasts as "Seven-Minute Fish Tales," though they were aired as "Romance Under the Waters." Higgins had hired a professional radio writer to do the scripts. But lacking a knowledge of biology, the writer soon ran into trouble. The staff scientists didn't fare much better with the scripts. They simply had no idea how to write for a nonscientific audience. Somehow Higgins managed to meet his weekly deadline for mailing new scripts to the radio stations. However, most of the programs made dull listening. Would Carson like to give it a try?

Of course, she would! Carson listened carefully as Higgins described the kind of stories and style of writing he wanted. He then outlined her first three assignments. For this part-time, temporary work, Higgins offered to pay her $1,000 a year, or $19.25 a week. During the depression, this was a good salary. When Carson returned with her first three scripts the following week, Higgins told her they would do just fine and gave her her next assignment.

Carson was excited to have a job. But she still worried about what would happen when she finished the scripts. Fortunately, the Bureau of Fisheries decided that the radio scripts could be turned into a brochure. Higgins asked Carson to rewrite and edit the broadcast material, giving it a good readable style. While Carson was busy with this task, she learned that the bureau would be giving an examination for the job of junior aquatic biologist. An aquatic biologist studies creatures that live in the water. The examination was part of the civil service procedure for filling any vacant government post permanently. Carson decided to take the examination. She was the only woman who did so, and she came out with the highest score.

On August 17, 1936, Carson joined the Bureau of Fisheries as a full-time employee at $2,000 a year, or $38.48 a week. She was twenty-nine years old. After eighteen months she would be eligible for a small raise based on the length of time she had served. Higgins requested that she be assigned to his office. For a lover of nature like Carson, being cooped up in an office all day was less than ideal. The bureau's offices were located on the first floor of a huge government office building in Washington, D.C. The only windows faced on an interior courtyard with a skylight. One day, as Carson trained her eyes upward, trying to get a glimpse of the sky, she remarked to a co-worker, "it's like working in the bottom of a well."

But working in the bottom of a well was better than no work at all—especially since another family tragedy had added to Carson's responsibilities. In 1936, after a long illness, her older sister, Marian, died at the age of forty. Earlier, Marian and her husband had divorced. She left behind two grade-school-age children, Marian Virginia Williams and Marjorie Louise Williams. Maria Carson felt that the girls should come and live with Rachel and herself, and Rachel agreed.

The Carsons moved out of the house on Stemmer's Run

into a two-story house in a modest neighborhood in Silver Spring, Maryland. The rent was higher, but they needed the extra room. Also, Silver Spring was an easier commute into Washington for Carson than Stemmer's Run had been.

When Carson had finished editing the "fish-tales" booklet for Higgins, he asked her to write an introduction to it. Carson worked long and hard on the introduction. But when she showed it to Higgins, he handed it back with the words, "I don't think it will do." Then with a twinkle in his eye, he advised her to send it to *The Atlantic Monthly*.

Carson was flabbergasted. *The Atlantic Monthly* was the country's most prestigious magazine. It dated back to the years before the Civil War. Since then, the magazine had published such major authors as Ralph Waldo Emerson, Henry David Thoreau, John Greenleaf Whittier, and James Russell Lowell. Carson found it hard to believe her little piece could compare with anything from the pens of these literary giants. She put the manuscript away and turned to the task of writing a suitable introduction for the "fish-tales" booklet.

On a more modest scale, however, Carson had already begun to sell articles to the Sunday magazine section of the *Baltimore Sun*. The headline of her first article was "It'll Be Shad-Time Soon—and Chesapeake Bay Fishermen Hope for Better Luck This Season." In it, Carson pointed out that there were several reasons for the "poor luck" of shad fishermen. One reason was the destructive methods used in commercial fishing. Another had to do with the pollution, or dirtying, of the water. Factories and towns and cities dumped so much waste material into the Chesapeake Bay that fish had a hard time surviving. When Carson wrote these words, few Americans were concerned about the problem of pollution.

39

For her *Baltimore Sun* articles, Carson usually didn't receive more than ten or fifteen dollars. But the extra money came in handy.

One day in 1937 Carson decided to take a chance with her "fish-tales" manuscript. She made a few changes suggested by Higgins and titled the piece "Undersea." Then she mailed it to *The Atlantic Monthly.* Six weeks later, Carson received a check for seventy-five dollars and the thrilling news that her piece would appear in the September 1937 issue.

The opening lines of "Undersea" showed Carson's gift for writing about the sea in an extremely vivid manner:

Who has known the ocean? Neither you nor I, with our earth-bound senses, know the foam and surge of the tide that beats over the crab hiding under the seaweed of his tide-pool home; or the lilt of the long, slow swells of midocean, where shoals of wandering fish prey and are preyed upon, and the dolphin breaks the waves to breathe the upper atmosphere.

After this promising beginning, Carson describes each part of the ocean in greater detail. She starts with the teeming life of the tide pools—pools of water left by the retreating ocean tides. In these "seas in miniature," sponges, starfish, and sea anemone make their home.

Next, Carson moves to the surface waters of the sea. She calls these surface waters "ocean pastures," because they are inhabited by millions of tiny plants and animals, as well as schools of full-sized fish. Carson then takes readers one hundred feet below the surface. In this twilight place, "spine-studded urchins . . . tumble over the sands," and "mollusks lie with slightly opened shells." Finally Carson's "underwater traveler" reaches the dark, icy depths of the sea. Here small, fierce fish with "gaping, tooth-studded jaws" move to and fro.

Carson wrote about the sea from an ecological point of view. Ecology is the study of living things in relation to their environment and to each other. At the time, few people had heard of the word *ecology* or understood the idea behind it.

Carson, however, showed how sea water receives from earth and air the materials that nourish the plant life of the ocean. This plant life, in turn, provides food for millions of tiny animals. Schools of fish feed upon these tiny animals. Humans catch and eat the fish. Every year, Carson pointed out, humans remove from the sea nearly 30 billion pounds of fish. In the end, though, every living thing of the ocean, whether plant or animal, returns to the water the materials used to create it. Thus, according to Carson, the life span of a particular plant or animal is only a brief moment in a cycle of endless change.

For Rachel Carson, personally, much was to follow from this one brief, beautiful piece of writing.

CHAPTER

5

Blackfoot, Silverbar, and Scomber

Rachel Carson's mail had never contained anything so exciting. The letter arrived a few weeks after the publication of "Undersea." A bright-green seascape, showing a blue whale and a couple of sharks, decorated the envelope. Opening the letter, Carson discovered it was from Hendrik Van Loon. Van Loon was the author of a best-selling book, *The Story of Mankind,* published in 1921. He had found "Undersea" such fascinating reading that he thought Carson ought to expand it into a book. Van Loon had even called Quincy Howe, the editor-in-chief at the publishing company of Simon and Schuster and urged him to contact Carson. In fact, Carson had received a letter from Howe the week before. Already, too, Elmer Higgins had suggested Carson develop "Undersea" into a full-length book. Now a well-known author wanted to take Carson under his wing and see that the project was launched. She could hardly believe her good fortune.

Van Loon invited Carson to come to his home in Old Greenwich, Connecticut. He wanted to arrange a meeting with Quincy Howe. In mid-January 1938, Carson traveled to Old Greenwich. She spent two days with the Van Loons, and in the evening Howe and his wife came to dinner. Van Loon explained why he was so interested in Carson's article. He had crossed the ocean several times. Each time he had been struck by how lifeless it appeared. Yet he knew that under the surface the ocean brimmed with life and was curious to know more about it. When he read "Undersea," Van Loon decided that Carson was the person who could tell him what he wanted to know.

With Van Loon and Howe, Carson discussed her idea for a book that would describe the life of the seashore, the open sea, and the sea bottom. Both men were pleased with the plan. But before Carson could get a book contract with Simon and Schuster, she needed to develop her plan in more detail and even write a few chapters.

Carson worked on the book in the evenings after putting in an eight-hour day at the Bureau of Fisheries and on weekends. She did a great deal of research so the scientific facts in the book would be accurate. But she kept the project pretty much to herself. Only a few friends and co-workers even knew she was writing a book.

In February 1938, Carson asked Van Loon's help in getting an advance payment from Simon and Schuster. This would enable her to devote all her free time to working on the book. Otherwise, she would have to spend part of that time writing newspaper articles to bring in extra money. The advance would also pay for a trip south she wanted to make as part of her research.

By June, Carson still hadn't heard anything from Simon and Schuster. But she went ahead with her trip to the U.S.

Bureau of Fisheries station at Beaufort, North Carolina. Finally, after Simon and Schuster had seen one chapter and a full outline of the book, they sent a check for $250. The company would not, however, give Carson a book contract until its editors had seen several more chapters.

Early in 1940, Carson managed to finish five chapters, or about twenty-two thousand words. Maria Carson, now seventy-one but as energetic as ever, typed the manuscript. Then off it went to Simon and Schuster. The editors there were very enthusiastic. They sent Carson a contract. After she had signed and returned it, the publisher sent her another check for $250.

Carson was pleased to have a contract. Now, however, she had a specific deadline to meet. The completed manuscript was due in the hands of the publisher on December 31, 1940. Carson wrote slowly, taking great care with her choice of words. She rewrote pages over and over again until she was satisfied. A single page went into seven different drafts, or versions, before she decided it was right.

Carson often worked late into the night in a large bedroom that occupied the entire second floor of the Silver Spring house. Her only companions during these long, lonely hours were two Persian cats. Buzzie and Kito were the offspring of Mitzi, the cat her brother, Robert, had given her several years earlier. Buzzie liked to curl up on the pile of Carson's notes and manuscript pages. On one or two of the pages she sketched him about to fall asleep, then dozing on her work.

Throughout the last part of 1940, Carson corresponded with artists about illustrations for the book. She chose Howard Frech, the staff artist on the *Baltimore Sun,* to be the illustrator. She was very concerned that the illustrations be scientifically accurate. So she sent Frech lists of reference books to use.

Carson gave her book the title of *Under the Sea Wind* and dedicated it to her mother. She delivered the complete manuscript to Simon and Schuster on time. Almost a year later, when Carson received her author's copies from the publisher, she took one to Elmer Higgins at the Bureau of Fisheries. On the blank page inside the cover, Carson had written: "To Mr. Higgins, who started it all."

Under the Sea Wind was different from many other books about the sea. In the foreword, or introductory remarks, to the first edition, Carson described her goal. She wrote that she wanted "to make the sea and its life as vivid a reality for those who may read the book as it has become for me." To accomplish this, she decided to tell three stories dealing with the life of the shore, the open sea, and the sea bottom.

Carson needed a main character for the stories. However, no single creature lived in all these different parts of the sea. Finally she decided that the sea itself would be the main character. It was "the sense of the sea, holding the power of life and death over every one of its creatures from the largest to smallest," that would fill each page of the book.

Nevertheless, each of the three stories has its own set of main characters. In the first story, "The Edge of the Sea," the main characters are two shore birds, Blackfoot, the leader of the sanderling flock, and his mate, Silverbar. Every spring these birds make an 8,000-mile migration, or move, from their winter home in South America to their summer home in the Arctic.

When we first meet Blackfoot and Silverbar, they have stopped over at an island off North Carolina. Continuing on to the Arctic, the birds suffer an especially severe snowstorm that takes many lives. But once the storm is over, the birds are able to breed and raise their young during the short northern summer. In the fall, they set out on the long trip south again.

The hero of the second story, which deals with the life of the open sea, is a mackerel named Scomber. Scomber begins life as a tiny egg drifting helplessly on the surface of the great ocean. After a few months, he has grown into a three-inch-long fish with a torpedo-shaped body and scaly coat. He then makes his way into a sheltered New England harbor. Here he joins a school of several thousand young mackerel. In the fall, Scomber and the school of fish leave the safety of the harbor for the open sea, where they will spend the rest of their lives.

At each stage of his life, Scomber barely escapes death in the jaws of a variety of predators—animals that live by killing and eating other animals. In the beginning, the predators are tiny anchovies and shellfish not much bigger than Scomber himself. But as Scomber grows, so do his enemies. They range from a conger eel "as long as a man is tall" to five-hundred-pound tuna:

> As the tuna drove through the milling fish, panic and confusion spread. There was no escape before or behind, nor to right or left. There was none below, where the tuna were. Along with most of his fellows, Scomber climbed up and up. The water was paling as it thinned away above them. Scomber could feel the thudding water vibration of an enormous fish climbing behind him, faster than a small mackerel could climb. He felt the five-hundred-pound tuna graze his flank as it seized the fish swimming beside him. Then he was at the surface, and the tuna were still pursuing. He leaped

into the air, fell back, leaped again and again. In the air, birds stabbed at him with their beaks, for the spurting spray was a sign of feeding tuna that brought gulls hurrying to the spot. . . .

Now Scomber's leaps were shorter and more labored, and he was falling back with the heaviness of exhaustion. Twice he had barely escaped the jaws of a tuna and many times he had seen one of his companions seized by the attacking fish.

In the end, Scomber is saved, as he has often been before, when his attackers are themselves attacked. Twenty-foot killer whales attack the largest of the tuna, "falling upon it like a pack of wolves." Later, when Scomber is trapped in a huge fishing net, he escapes because razor-teethed dogfish slash holes in the net.

The third story has to do with a female eel named Anguilla. Born in the deep sea, Anguilla has spent her adult life in an inland pond. But now in her tenth spring she obeys an instinct stronger than hunger and sets out on a two-hundred-mile journey. This journey takes her back to the place where she was born and where she will die, leaving newborn eels to repeat her migration. By the next fall, these young eels, or elvers, have already reached the mouth of the bay through which Anguilla and her companions had traveled nearly a year before.

In her use of animals as distinct, named characters, Carson followed the example of the British nature writer Henry Williamson. Williamson's books included *Tarka the Otter* and *Salar the Salmon*. Carson admired the way Williamson entered into the lives of the otter and the salmon, how he saw with their eyes, and followed "the moving drama" of their everyday life.

Wherever possible, Carson used the scientific names for animals. Scomber, for example, is the scientific name of the mackerel. Sometimes, though, the scientific name for an animal was too long and difficult. So Carson used a name that described something about the way the animal looked, such as Blackfoot and Silverbar.

Carson wanted her readers to enter imaginatively into the lives of the sea creatures she described. This meant that readers had to give up many ideas related to human life. They had to learn to measure time not by the clock or calendar, but by light and darkness and the tides.

Carson also believed that the sea creatures' lives would become real to people only if people could connect the creatures' lives to their own. As a scientist, however, she had to be careful not to describe animals as if they were capable of human feelings and intelligence. In the foreword to the book, she explained: "I have spoken of a fish 'fearing' his enemies. . . not because I suppose a fish experiences fear in the same way that we do, but because I think he *behaves as though he were frightened.*" What in the fish is mainly a physical response is in people mental and emotional. But if the fish's behavior is to be understood, it must be described in words relating to human mental and emotional states.

The lives of the different creatures described in the book all involve a fierce struggle for survival. While Scomber narrowly escapes death on a number of occasions, other creatures aren't so lucky. Of one hundred thousand shad eggs that are laid, only one or two will live to grow into fish and lay eggs of their own. Yet, according to Carson, this is part of nature's plan. "By such ruthless selection," she writes, "the species are kept in check."

At one point in the story, porpoises kill a few mackerel "for sport." But this is the only instance Carson gives us of unnecessary killing in the animal world. Otherwise, she shows us that animals don't usually kill unless they are hungry. Thus in the book, a fox doesn't go after lemming mice, because he has just eaten a bird.

Carson also shows us that in nature nothing is wasted. First gulls, then fish crows and ghost crabs, and finally sand hoppers eat the small fish that fishermen have discarded on the beach. "For in the sea," Carson writes, "nothing is lost. One dies, another lives, as the precious elements of life are passed on and on in endless chains."

However, human beings sometimes upset this ecological balance, as Carson demonstrates. They overfish certain areas and shoot too many birds. Carson especially criticizes the "gunners defying the law for the fancied pleasure of stopping in full flight a brave and fiercely burning life." Elsewhere in the book, she refers to the great clouds of passenger pigeons that filled the skies before hunters caused them to become extinct, that is, die out altogether.

By this time, conservationists both in and outside the government had become alarmed at the tremendous slaughter of ducks and other waterfowl. They fought to protect these birds by setting limits on the number hunters could shoot and by limiting the hunting season. They also pushed for more wildlife refuges, where waterfowl could safely live and breed. In 1937, the U.S. Congress passed a new law to help wildlife conservation. The law levied a federal tax on sporting guns and ammunition. The government used this tax money to develop and restore wildlife areas all over the country.

Carson, however, didn't write *Under the Sea Wind* to attack hunting and fishing. Rather, she wanted to share her knowledge of and enthusiasm for the life of the sea with readers. But by getting us to enter imaginatively into the creatures' lives, Carson makes us care about their survival.

We become like the mackerel fisherman toward the end of Scomber's story. This particular fisherman wonders: "What had the eyes of the mackerel seen? Things he'd never see; places he'd never go." The fisherman even feels it's not quite right that a creature, which has survived the attacks of countless enemies in the ocean, should at last die on the deck of a mackerel boat. He imagines the fish diving to safety before the net has closed beneath them. Only after they have actually escaped, does he realize that for him, a fisherman, an hour of hard work has been wasted.

With its combination of dramatic storytelling and scientific accuracy, *Under the Sea Wind* won praise from scientists and nonscientists alike. One of the book's fans was Dr. William Beebe. A respected scientist, Beebe was the author of many nature books. He was also one of the first people to explore the ocean depths. In 1934, Beebe had descended one-half mile in a bathysphere—a steel diving sphere that was connected to the surface by cables.

Beebe said he had difficulty reading Carson's book aloud. But he also observed that he "thoroughly enjoyed every word" and that "Miss Carson's science cannot be questioned." He thought so well of the book that three years later, he included two chapters of it in his *Book of Naturalists*. This was a collection of some of the world's finest nature writing. Carson was pleased by the fact that Beebe's book "began with Aristotle [the ancient Greek philosopher] and ended with Carson." A warm friendship sprang up between Beebe and Carson.

Carson herself remained especially fond of *Under the Sea Wind*. Years later, she remarked that although the book had many faults, "I doubt that a writer ever quite recaptures the freshness of a first book."

Unfortunately, *Under the Sea Wind* came out at the worst possible time. Simon and Schuster published the book on November 1, 1941. A little more than a month later, on December 7, 1941, Japanese bombers attacked the U.S. naval base at Pearl Harbor, Hawaii.

When this happened, World War II had already been raging for two years. The war pitted Germany, Italy, and Japan against Great Britain and France, as well as a host of less powerful nations. The United States had supplied Great Britain and its allies with weapons and other supplies. But so far, the nation had kept out of the actual fighting. Now, however, the U.S. Congress declared war on Japan. A few days later, Germany and Italy declared war on the United States.

As Americans focused their attention on the war, Carson's beautiful book about the sea was all but forgotten. In the first year, only 1,348 copies were sold. Six years later, the total sales remained under 1,600. Carson's earnings from the book were less than $1,000. Little wonder that she advised a friend and fellow author to write magazine articles instead of books. The latter, Carson explained, simply didn't pay.

But the thirty-four-year-old author had little time for regrets. Along with the rest of the country, she was soon caught up in the war effort.

CHAPTER

6

Conservation During and After the War

For Rachel Carson, the war brought promotions, a move, and new work. In May 1942, she became assistant to the chief of the Office of Information in the Fish and Wildlife Service. Two years before, the Bureau of Fisheries in the Department of Commerce had been combined with the Biological Survey in the Department of Agriculture. These two agencies became the Fish and Wildlife Service under the Department of the Interior.

Carson was one of the first two women ever hired by the Fish and Wildlife Service for a nonclerical job. As an employee of the new agency, she came into contact with a wider range of conservationists. These people were concerned with preserving the nation's birds, mammals, and other wildlife, as well as its fish. The director of the Fish and Wildlife Service was Ira N. Gabrielson, former chief of the Biological Survey. Before the war, Gabrielson had pressed for more wildlife refuges. He was particularly concerned with protecting migrating water birds.

World War II led to a slowdown of the drive for more wildlife areas. The nation threw its resources—natural and human—into the war effort. In August 1942, the Fish and Wildlife Service and many of its staff moved to Chicago. They went to make room in Washington for the newly created wartime government agencies. From that summer until the following spring, Carson and her mother and nieces lived in Evanston, Illinois, a suburb of Chicago. Then they moved back to Washington.

Carson's main job during the war had to do with getting Americans to eat more fish. The government sent hundreds of thousands of tons of meat overseas to feed soldiers of the United States and its allies. So there were shortages at home. Families had to use such substitutes as buffalo, reindeer, and moose for familiar meats, or they had to turn to fish.

Between 1943 and 1945, Carson wrote four pamphlets, describing sixty-five fresh-water and salt-water fish and a dozen kinds of shellfish. The idea wasn't just to get Americans to eat more fish but to popularize little-known seafoods. "Each of the millions of people who buy and eat fish," Carson wrote, "can play an active part in conservation by utilizing a greater variety of seafood." She felt that people would enjoy the new seafoods more if they knew something about the creatures from which they came. She presented these sea creatures as individuals, each with its own flavor, food value, habits, and migrations.

Although these were factual pamphlets written for a practical purpose, they contain some passages of fine writing. Newspaper and magazine editors, as well as radio broadcasters, used the pamphlets to help persuade meat-eating Americans to switch to fish. Carson herself remained

53

unconvinced, however. Years later, the author who wrote so beautifully about the sea confessed to a dislike of seafood.

On weekends and in the evenings, Carson turned to another kind of writing. She had never found it easy to support the household on her modest government salary. She decided to take her own advice and try writing for magazines like the *Reader's Digest* that paid the highest rates for articles.

Late in 1944, Carson "broke into" the *Digest* with a story about bats and their use of "radar" to avoid obstacles in the dark. For this one article, she received $500—about half her total earnings on her first book. The U.S. Navy liked the piece so much that it decided to reprint it for recruiting purposes. Carson also sold articles to other major magazines, such as *Collier's, Coronet, Transatlantic,* and *Nature Magazine.*

However, as her government job became more demanding, Carson had less time for own writing. To a friend, Carson confided that if she could choose what seemed to her the ideal existence, it would be just to live by writing.

As a writer and editor of government publications, Carson set high standards for herself and others. She had little patience with shoddy work or time wasting. Ever polite in her official dealings with writers, she blew off steam in private when they failed to meet her standards.

Carson's good friend and co-worker Shirley Briggs, who joined the Fish and Wildlife Service in 1945, recalled that "her qualities of zest and humor made even the dull stretches. . .a matter for quiet fun." Carson, Briggs, and a few others in the service would gather over sandwiches at noon and for tea later in the day. They laughed about the endless rules and silly official statements that could make working for a large government agency difficult.

Sometimes Carson and her co-workers resorted to practical jokes like the so-called "Cookbook Hoax." A woman in the Chicago office of the Information Section had put together a very poor publication on the cooking of wildlife. Carson and her group made up a telegram to the woman supposedly from a feature writer for a big New York magazine. The telegram said the writer and a photographer were coming out to do an illustrated article. The article would include photos of a special dish—"field mice for twelve" served with mushrooms and white wine. Carson and her friends gave up the hoax after a lawyer friend told them they could be sent to jail for sending a telegram under a false name. But all agreed that they had almost as much fun imagining the scene as they would have if the hoax had actually come off.

Carson's family also appreciated her sense of humor. To her niece Virginia, she seemed more like an older sister and was "a lot of fun." At the same time, Carson was someone her nieces felt they could turn to in time of trouble.

Carson herself later remembered these years in Washington as carefree ones. Her mother did the housework and prepared all the meals. (Carson hated cooking.) Her mother was also on hand to look after Carson's nieces if she wanted to go away for the weekend or attend a party in the evening. There were lots of parties. People gathered at each others' homes to talk and simply have a good time. According to Shirley Briggs, "Ray," as friends called her, enjoyed different sorts of people, and was always eager to meet new ones.

Carson had both male and female friends. She did not, however, become romantically involved with any one man. Friends who knew both Carson and her mother well felt that Maria Carson didn't want her daughter to marry. Her mother's influence may indeed have been a factor in Carson's not marrying. But Carson herself may also have

55

preferred to remain single. She never mentioned any particular man she was interested in. Nor did she express a strong desire to marry. Years later, when an interviewer asked her why she had never married, Carson replied, "I didn't have time."

Carson and Shirley Briggs both enjoyed bird-watching, hiking, and exploring the outdoors. Armed with binoculars, they went on bird walks in parks around Washington with other members of the local Audubon Society. Founded in 1905, the National Audubon Society is one of the oldest and largest nationwide conservation organizations in the world. The society takes its name from John James Audubon, the famous American bird artist and naturalist, or student of nature.

On one of their walks, Carson and Briggs noticed a fellow bird-watcher who looked familiar. The young man looked like the picture they had seen of Louis J. Halle. Halle was the author of a birding book called *Spring in Washington*. Carson had enjoyed this book a great deal. Now she was delighted to discover that the man on the path before them was, indeed, Louis J. Halle.

Later, their mutual friend Edwin Way Teale formally introduced Halle and Carson. She asked Halle's advice on how to develop a good writing style. After Carson had become a best-selling author, Halle remembered this conversation with embarrassment. He felt he should have been the one to listen while she did the talking. But it wasn't Carson's way to put herself forward. She preferred to remain in the background, listening and learning.

Carson and Briggs also went on daylong and overnight trips with the Audubon Society. In October 1945, they journeyed to the Hawk Mountain Sanctuary in Pennsylvania to watch the famous fall migration of the birds. Even in the

Rachel Carson on Hawk Mountain. Rachel Carson and her friend,
Shirley Briggs, traveled to the Hawk Mountain Sanctuary in
Pennsylvania.

mountains, Carson thought of the sea. Watching the streams race down the mountainsides, she remembered that these waters would eventually flow into the ocean. She also found reminders of the ancient seas that had once spread over the land. And lying on her back with half-closed eyes, she felt herself to be "at the bottom of another ocean—an ocean of air on which the hawks are sailing."

On another trip to the Florida Everglades for the Fish and Wildlife Service, Carson also had a strong "sense of the sea on land." The watery grasslands of the Everglades are now a national park. At the time, though, the Fish and Wildlife Service managed the area.

Carson and Briggs decided to visit the Everglades when they learned of a man with a "glades buggy." The man had never taken a woman into the swamps. He tried to persuade them that it would be very uncomfortable. But when they persisted, he gave in. The "glades buggy" turned out to be a vehicle like a tractor. It had six pairs of very large wheels and an exposed engine. The engine blasted heat on them throughout their journey.

But the scenery proved worth the discomfort. The immense space of the Everglades, combined with the flatness of the land and the expanse of sky, reminded Carson of the sea. Even the low hills of palmetto and other trees that rose up here and there made her think of islands in the ocean. Finally, the whole area "appeared as trackless and as lacking in landmarks as the sea."

Fortunately, their guide knew the way. The only trouble was that he wasn't sure they had enough gas to get back. Also, every time they stopped, clouds of mosquitoes attacked them. Carson and Briggs were very relieved when near dusk they came out of the Everglades to find the game warden and Fish and Wildlife Service patrolmen waiting for them.

By the end of World War II in August 1945, Carson had become increasingly restless with her job. She had been with the Fish and Wildlife Service for nearly ten years now and was eager for a change. With the encouragement of Quincy Howe and Lincoln Schuster at Simon and Schuster, she applied for a job as an editor at the *Reader's Digest*. She also tried the National Audubon Society and the New York Zoological Society, where her friend Dr. William Beebe was the person in charge of the study of birds. But there were no openings available at any of these places.

The following summer, Carson left the office for a vacation in a place that was to have an important influence on her life and writing. In July 1946, she and her family rented a cabin on the Sheepscot River near Boothbay Harbor, Maine.

The cabin was so near the river that if Carson had jumped out the windows on one side, she would have landed in the water. The only sounds were the lapping of the water, the cries of gulls, herons, and ospreys, and sometimes the tolling of a buoy bell. Carson loved exploring the nearby tide pools and simply lying on her back watching the birds fly overhead. She wrote Shirley Briggs that her greatest ambition was to buy a place in the area and spend a lot of time there.

Fortunately, the situation at work had improved. With the war over, the Fish and Wildlife Service returned its attention to the wildlife refuge system. By the late 1940s, there were some three hundred such refuges. About two hundred of these were for the protection of migrating water birds. The new director of the service, Albert M. Day, decided to publish a series of twelve illustrated booklets on the wildlife refuges. He put Carson in charge of the series, which was called "Conservation in Action."

59

The booklets were timely, because new threats to wildlife and wild areas were beginning to appear. In the postwar years, the country underwent a population explosion. Once the Great Depression had ended, people had more money to support families. Also, when soldiers returned from the war, they were eager to start families. All these new families needed places to live. The result was a building boom. Most new houses were built outside of cities in the suburbs. Thousands of miles of new highways connected the sprawling suburbs with nearby cities.

The "Conservation in Action" booklets were designed to acquaint people with the various wildlife refuges and to serve as guidebooks. Most important of all, the booklets urged Americans to join the fight to preserve homes for wildlife. "Wild creatures, like men, need a place to live," Carson wrote in the introduction to the series. (Along with many other writers at that time, Carson used the word *men* or *man* for human beings as a group.) "As civilization creates cities, builds highways, and drains marshes it takes away, little by little, the land that is suitable for wildlife. And as their spaces dwindle, the wildlife populations themselves dwindle."

Carson went on to say that all the people in the country had a stake in wildlife conservation. For commercial fishermen and trappers, the stake was financial. For people who liked to hunt, fish, or photograph nature, conservation meant preserving a favorite form of recreation. Still others got as much enjoyment from observing nature as they did from looking at the artworks or listening to music. "But for all the people, the preservation of wildlife and wildlife habitat means also the preservation of the basic resources of the earth, which men, as well as animals, must have in order to live."

For Carson, the fun part of producing this series was the opportunity to visit the various wildlife refuges. In April 1946, she and Shirley Briggs went to Assateague Island along the Maryland-Virginia coast to gather material for the first booklet. They took pictures, climbed the lighthouse, dug clams, and went on a wild ride with the refuge manager to rescue two horses that had gotten stuck in the mud.

Most of the trips Carson took in connection with the series were along the Atlantic coast. But one took her as far west as Oregon. She told a friend that she wished she could spend all her time doing this sort of thing.

Carson saw to it that the "Conservation in Action" booklets set a new standard of excellence in government publications. By 1949 she had become editor-in-chief of Fish and Wildlife Service publications. A staff of six assisted her. Carson worked with authors in planning and writing their manuscripts. She also reviewed all work that was submitted, and supervised the editing and preparation of manuscripts for the printer. Carson herself described her work as that of a small publishing house.

The refuge series and other publications kept Carson very busy. Nevertheless, she found time for a project of her own. Every few days, her co-worker, wildlife artist Bob Hines, brought Carson stacks of scientific books from the local libraries. Hines piled them on the backseat of Carson's car when she drove home at the end of the afternoon. A few days later, he exchanged the books for a new load. Late into the night, Carson studied these highly technical volumes, taking notes for the great book about the sea she was determined to write.

7

The Sea Around Us

Rachel Carson began work on her new book about the sea in 1948 when she was forty-one years old. But in a sense, she had been preparing to write this book her entire life. The book combined her childhood fascination with the sea with the vast amount of knowledge she had gained as a marine biologist.

Her first summer at Woods Hole, Carson had watched the ocean tides rise and fall and the waves crash against the shore after a storm. At Woods Hole, too, she first became aware of the unseen currents, or waters that move about the ocean in streams. After a storm, Carson observed masses of brown seaweed that she knew had come from tropical, or much warmer, waters. She also observed tropical creatures like the beautiful Portuguese man-of-war, a type of jellyfish. The Gulf Stream had carried the jellyfish and seaweed all the way to the Massachusetts coast. The Gulf Stream is a current of warm water. It starts in the Gulf of Mexico and flows in a northeasterly direction parallel to the U.S. coast.

Carson had also studied the sea at the excellent library of the Marine Biological Laboratory at Woods Hole. She spent hours seeking answers in books and scientific journals to the questions that filled her mind.

In the years since Carson had first begun her studies, knowledge about the sea increased. World War II, in particular, brought a number of advances in oceanography. Oceanography is the scientific study of the oceans. During the war, the U.S. government launched many military operations involving ships or submarines. The success of these operations often depended on the military's ability to predict the action of ocean tides, currents, and waves. Because of her position with the government, Carson had sat in on top-level discussions of the effects of the ocean on military operations.

To help the military understand the sea better, scientists developed new instruments like the wave recorder. It tells scientists where in the ocean particular waves were created, the strength of the winds that produced them, and how fast a storm is moving.

Another instrument was an echo-sounding device. This instrument sends back echoes from the sea bottom that provide information about its depth. By taking soundings over different areas, scientists can trace the shape of the ocean bottom. In the past, oceanographers had believed that aside from a few known mountains and trenches, the ocean floor was a large, level plain. Now they discovered that it was actually quite rugged.

Now, too, scientists were able to remove layers of sediment from the ocean bottom with long tubes called corers. These layers of sand, mud, and other materials had

63

settled on the ocean floor over hundreds of millions of years. They provided valuable information about the history of both sea and land.

One unusual discovery came about entirely by accident. During the war, the U.S. Navy set up a network of underwater listening devices called hydrophones along parts of the coast. The navy wanted to protect against attack by enemy submarines. Biologists listening to these devices heard an astonishing mixture of sounds, including whistles and squeals, mewing and chirps, and a crackling, sizzling noise. Fish, shrimp, and porpoises were responsible for this uproar. So much for the widely held belief that the sea was a silent place.

These and other discoveries thrilled Carson. The more she learned, the more she was impressed by how much human beings depended on the sea. She believed that people would become even more dependent on the ocean if they went on destroying the land.

The time seemed ripe to put all the new information about the sea together in a book. It would be "a book for anyone who has looked upon the ocean with wonder." It would also be a book that Carson herself had looked for on the library shelves and never found. She wanted her book to be "easily understood and imaginatively appealing to the reader untrained in science."

The sea was a vast and complicated subject. Carson knew that to try to deal with it by herself would be almost impossible. So she turned to other experts for help. She wrote letters to oceanographers all over the world and discussed the book with specialists in different areas of study.

Three people were particularly helpful to Carson. One was Henry B. Bigelow, a world-famous oceanographer at Harvard University. Another was Robert Cushman Murphy, the curator, or person in charge, of the bird department at the American Museum of Natural History. In the course of his nature studies, Murphy had gone on the last of the whaling voyages under sail in the Antarctic. He had also traveled to South America to study the mysterious Humboldt Current and the ocean birds there.

Thor Heyerdahl, a Norwegian scientist, was the third person who helped Carson. In the summer of 1947, Heyerdahl and five companions set out on a remarkable journey. On a light balsa-wood raft, they drifted 4,300 miles across the Pacific Ocean from the coast of Peru to the Tuamotu Islands in eastern Polynesia. Heyerdahl wanted to test his theory that the original inhabitants of Polynesia might have come from South America by raft. During his 101-day ocean voyage, Heyerdahl had a unique opportunity to study the life of the surface waters, especially at night. He shared his observations with Carson. Heyerdahl also wrote a best-selling book, *Kon-Tiki* (1950), about the trip.

In all, Carson consulted more than a thousand printed sources while she was researching her book. In addition to wartime studies of the ocean, she found the books in the series "Coast Pilots and Sailing Directions" fascinating reading. These were guides for mariners published by the government. Carson especially enjoyed the sailing directions for the least known, least traveled coasts, as well as the ones for dangerous waters, like those off Alaska and Norway. Reading the guides gave her a sense of the sea's power and its ability to act in unexpected ways. The guides also reminded her of how much humans had yet to learn about the sea.

By the summer of 1948, Carson had put together a list of possible chapters for her book. She now decided to find a literary agent. A literary agent is a professional who looks after the interests of writers in their dealings with publishers. After interviewing several agents, Carson selected Marie Rodell in New York.

Rodell's first task was to find a publisher for Carson's book. Simon and Schuster, the publisher of *Under the Sea Wind*, would have been a possibility if that book had sold much better than it did. Instead, Rodell tried another publishing house and was turned down. The editors there didn't think they could make a decision about such a huge project on the basis of just an outline and a sample chapter.

Four months later, Carson completed a rough draft of about one-third of the book. Rodell submitted these chapters to Philip Vaudrin, the executive editor of Oxford University Press. Vaudrin liked what he saw. In May 1949 he sent Carson a book contract.

Already in April, Carson had met with Dr. William Beebe in New York. Beebe convinced her that she couldn't finish the book without getting under water. He was so enthusiastic about the idea that he had Carson practically on her way to Bermuda, where he himself had gone diving.

That July, Carson's "Great Undersea Adventure," as she jokingly called it, took place in Florida. She was neither an experienced swimmer nor diver. So Carson in diving helmet with lead weights on her feet went only fifteen feet below the surface. It was enough, however, to make her a bit nervous, but also to give her a good look at life undersea.

Later that month, Carson went on a much more rugged adventure. In the course of her work, Carson had sometimes gone out for short cruises on fishing boats or research vessels. Now she took a real deep-sea voyage.

At the time, the Fish and Wildlife Service operated a research vessel, the *Albatross III*, on the famous fishing grounds known as Georges Bank. Georges Bank is located about 200 miles east of Boston and south of Nova Scotia. Some of the popular commercial fish like cod were becoming scarce there. The service wanted to find out why. The *Albatross* made regular trips from Woods Hole to Georges Bank to count the fish population there. It did this by fishing in a systematic way at a series of different locations.

When Carson applied for permission to go on the *Albatross*, no woman had ever been on board. Carson's male co-workers had to sign the papers enabling her to go. They didn't like the idea of her being the only woman on a ship with fifty-some men. Finally, however, they decided that *two* women might be all right. Carson arranged for Marie Rodell to accompany her. Rodell joked that she would write a piece about her experiences entitled "I Was a Chaperone on a Fishing Boat."

Carson and Rodell had no sooner climbed on board than the ship's officers began telling them horror stories. The officers advised them to always hang on to something, because the water coming over the decks could bang them around a lot. The officers also told them that since the *Albatross* was long and narrow, it rolled like a canoe in the waves, making everyone violently seasick. The men gleefully described various unpleasant accidents that sometimes occurred in handling the heavy fishing gear. Finally, Carson and Rodell would have to put up with bad food and the daily and nightly racket made by the fishing process.

Carson and Rodell quickly discovered that the officers were right about the noise. The first night at sea, a loud crash awakened them around midnight. It sounded as if another vessel had rammed into their boat. Terrible bangs, clunks, and rumbles followed the crash.

What the two women heard was the trawl, or huge cone-shaped net, being dropped into the water. The net was attached to the ship by two long cables. It dragged the ocean floor, scraping up anything lying on the bottom or swimming just above it. After about a half hour of trawling, as this type of fishing is called, big winches, or cranks, hauled in the cables. As the cables came on board, they were wound onto steel drums.

Carson and Rodell realized they were in for ten more nights of this racket. The next morning, the grinning officers asked them if they had heard anything during the night. Rodell replied that they thought they heard a mouse, but were too sleepy to bother. After two nights, they did, in fact, learn to sleep through the uproar "like old salts."

Sometimes Carson and Rodell stayed on deck at night to watch the fishing. The experience made a big impression on Carson. The sight of the net coming in with its load of fish gave her a sense of sea depths that she had never had before. No two catches were exactly alike. The most interesting ones came from deeper areas. Then the trawl brought up larger fish. Because of the sudden change in water pressure as the net was coming up, some of the fish were greatly swollen. They drifted out of the net, but couldn't swim down again. Sharks moved in to kill these fish. Carson felt there was something very beautiful about the sharks. When some of the men got out rifles to kill the sharks for sport, Carson wrote that it "really hurt" her.

The fog that blanketed Georges Bank made Carson aware of the Gulf Stream's power. A hundred miles of cold Atlantic Ocean water lay between Georges Bank and the Gulf Stream. But winds blowing from the south carried the current's "warm breath" to the fishing grounds. The combination of warm air and cold water meant endless fog.

The experience of the night sea on a small boat far from land was perhaps the most unforgettable of all. Standing on deck, Carson could just make out the huge shapes of waves rolling around the tiny wood-and-steel "island" of the boat. At these moments, she was, in her own words, "conscious as never before that ours is a water world dominated by the immensity of the ocean."

Back on land, Carson struggled to find both the time and money that would enable her to complete the book. That fall, she had to look for and then move into another house in Silver Spring. The illness of one of her nieces also cut into precious after-work and weekend hours that Carson would otherwise have devoted to writing.

Fortunately, in October, Carson was able to take a month-long leave without pay from her government job. On the recommendation of Dr. Beebe and Edwin Way Teale, she had received a Eugene F. Saxton Memorial Fellowship of $2,250. The fellowships were intended to help creative writers complete worthwhile projects.

Now that she no longer had to go into work, Carson began to keep the same hours as her cat, Muffin. She worked late into the night, then slept late in the morning. While she worked, her cat amused itself by cuffing at the keys of her typewriter and watching them spring back.

To unwind after a long night's work, Carson often read a few pages of one of her favorite books. She kept a volume of the *Journal* of the nineteenth-century American nature writer Henry David Thoreau by her bedside. She enjoyed the nature writing of the British author Richard Jeffries, too. Other favorites were *Moby Dick* by Herman Melville, *The Sea and the Jungle* by H. M. Tomlinson, and *The Outermost House* by Henry Beston. Beston's book was the story of a year the author had spent living by himself in a small house on an isolated Cape Cod beach.

Carson also admired the sea books of the Polish-born

English novelist Joseph Conrad. She especially liked the descriptions of the sea in one of Conrad's less known works, *The Mirror of the Sea.*

Carson's leave put her badly behind at work. No sooner had she returned to the office than she was overwhelmed by everything that needed to be done. The only way to catch up was to take office work home nights and weekends, which, of course, took away from her writing time. That spring, she was too busy to go on a single bird walk.

In 1950, with her deadline for turning in the manuscript only months away, Carson learned that Mary Skinker was dying of cancer. She borrowed plane fare and flew to Chicago, so she could be at the bedside of her friend and former teacher.

Around this time, too, Carson and her editor finally settled on a title for her book. They had considered numerous possibilities. These included *Return to the Sea, Mother Sea, The Story of the Sea,* and even *Sea Without End.* Friends and relatives humorously suggested *Out of My Depth* and *Carson at Sea.* At her wit's end, Carson remembered an early candidate, *The Sea Around Us.* Both she and her editor agreed it was the best choice.

Carson delivered the manuscript of *The Sea Around Us* to her publisher early in July 1950. Once again her mother, who was now eighty-one, typed the final version. With the manuscript out of her hands, Carson felt both a sense of accomplishment and a sense of loss. Now that the actual writing was done, she was concerned with the design and manufacture of the book. She wanted *The Sea Around Us* to look attractive to readers.

Money troubles continued to bother Carson. She couldn't expect any financial return from the book until it was published and began to sell. To help tide Carson over,

Marie Rodell tried to sell chapters to magazines in advance of publication. Rejections of book manuscripts and articles are common in the field of publishing. Nevertheless, Rodell was surprised when nearly twenty major magazines turned down the chapters submitted to them. The magazines included *The Atlantic Monthly*, which had published "Undersea" twelve years before.

Finally, though, Rodelll was able to sell a chapter to the *Yale Review*. The publication of this chapter before the end of 1950 won Carson the George Westinghouse Science Writing Award. Given by the American Association for the Advancement of Science, this $1,000 prize was for the "finest example of science writing in any American magazine in 1950." Rodell also sold a chapter to *Science Digest*.

But most thrilling of all was the response from *The New Yorker*. Carson's material was different from anything the magazine had published in its long and distinguished career. However, editor William Shawn was convinced that Carson's book would be a great one.

The New Yorker ended up printing half the book as a "biography" of the ocean in its "Profile" department. This part of the magazine was normally reserved for the life stories of remarkable people. *The New Yorker* received more enthusiastic letters from readers about this "profile" than anything else it had ever printed. The profile, in turn, helped launch the book.

The magazine paid Carson several thousand dollars for the right to reprint parts of *The Sea Around Us*. The sum was almost as much as Carson received for a full year's work for the government!

As excitement about the book mounted, its shy author found herself thrust into the public eye. Carson's publisher was planning a big party in Washington to celebrate the book's publication. In June 1951, shortly before the party and publication, Carson slipped off to a favorite beach in Beaufort, North Carolina. She wore out the seat of her pants on the barnacle-covered rocks and became so sunburned she was glad she hadn't bought a pink dress for the party.

On July 2, *The Sea Around Us* rolled off the press and into the hands of eager readers. The Book-of-the-Month Club offered the book to its members as an alternate selection. The Book-of-the-Month Club is a commercial organization that sends and sells selected books to its members at regular intervals and often at a discount. *Reader's Digest* also published a shortened version.

The demand was such that Oxford University Press quickly had to print more copies. By the end of the month, *The Sea Around Us* had made the *New York Times* best-seller list. It remained there for eighty-six weeks. Foreign publishers decided to put out editions of the book. Eventually, it appeared in thirty-two languages.

Suddenly, everybody was talking about Rachel Carson. People wanted to know what she looked like, how old she was, and how she had happened to discover the sea. Carson's publisher had failed to put a picture of her on the book jacket. So some—male readers especially—thought she must be a man, because only a man could have dealt with such a scientific topic. Others assumed she must be old and gray. How else could she have gathered all the information that went into her book? One man even wrote Carson that she was just what he was looking for in a wife—except for her advanced age!

People who actually met Carson or saw pictures of her in magazines were quite surprised. One magazine writer observed that Carson's "slender prettiness does not suggest the seagoing buccaneer."

Rachel Carson at Woods Hole, Massachusetts, in 1951. In that year
The Sea Around Us *was published and quickly became a best-seller.*

Wherever Carson went, people fought to get a glimpse of her. Once when she was sitting under the hair drier at a beauty parlor, the owner came over, turned off the drier, and told her there was someone who wanted to meet her.

73

Another time, Carson and her mother were staying at a motel when there was a knock on the door early in the morning. After her mother opened the door, a determined woman rushed in and presented Carson, who was still in bed, with two books she wanted autographed.

Being famous wasn't easy for a quiet, retiring person like Carson. She lost twenty pounds during all the excitement over *The Sea Around Us.*

What made the book such a big success? Once again, Carson successfully combined scientific accuracy with a writing style that was both vivid and easily understood by nonscientists. This was very important, because at the time few people other than a small number of scientists had actually seen many of the things Carson described.

Today, TV programs about the ocean and undersea life are common. In 1951, however, such programs didn't exist. Television was still a relatively new invention, and undersea photography was just being pioneered. Also, divers lacked the sophisticated equipment that today enables them to descend to depths of more than six miles below the ocean's surface. Divers also lacked the underwater laboratories, or habitats, that enable them to remain below the surface for several months at a time.

Carson's task, then, was to create strong, clear word pictures that would help people visualize what they couldn't otherwise see. Sometimes she does this by making comparisons with things on land. For example, she describes the movement of materials down to the ocean floor as "the long snowfall":

When I think of the floor of the deep sea, the single, overwhelming fact that possesses my imagination is the accumulation of sediments. I see always the steady, unremitting downward drift of materials from above, flake upon flake, layer upon layer—a drift that has continued for hundreds of millions of years, that will go on as long as there are seas and continents.

Carson also managed to pack a remarkable amount of information into two hundred-some pages. The first part of the book, "Mother Sea," describes how the oceans and the life they support were formed. It also describes the nature of the sea and the changing relationships between land and sea. Part II, "The Restless Sea," deals with the forces that act on the oceans—winds, moon and sun, and the rotation of the earth. Part III, "Man and the Sea About Him," describes the effect of the oceans on human life.

Carson shows how the sea affects the world's climate. She also shows how it provides people with many important minerals. For example, without magnesium from the sea, the United States couldn't have built the airplanes it used in World War II. Each one of those airplanes contained about a half ton of the metal magnesium.

The Sea Around Us brings out certain ideas that were important in *Under the Sea Wind.* One major theme is that sea life consists of a series of interlocking relationships. According-ing to Carson, what happens to a diatom, or tiny sea plant, on the water's surface may have an effect on a cod lying on the ledge of some rocky canyon six hundred feet below. She views the sea as a balanced system, in which everything has many uses. "Nothing is wasted in the sea;" she writes, "every particle of material is used over and over again, first by one creature, then by another."

Unfortunately, human beings sometimes disturb this ecological balance. In the chapter "The Birth of an Island,"

75

Carson describes how people have brought about "disastrous changes" on islands in the oceans.

Because these islands were isolated from the mainland, they developed different kinds of plants and animals from those found on the continents. When human introduced animals like goats, hogs, and rats onto remote islands, they destroyed the islands' unique plant and animal life. For instance, when people brought rabbits onto the Pacific island of Laysan, the rabbits ate up all the vegetation and turned the island into a sandy desert.

"In a reasonable world," Carson concludes, "men would have treated these islands as precious possessions, as natural museums filled with beautiful and curious works of creation, valuable beyond price because nowhere in the world are they duplicated." Instead, the result has been the tragic loss of unique species.

Nevertheless, Carson expresses the belief that human beings can't control or change the ocean in the same way that they have "subdued and plundered" the continents. At the book's close, she writes:

> For the sea lies all about us. The commerce of all lands must cross it. . . . The continents themselves dissolve and pass to the sea, in grain after grain of eroded land. So the rains that rose from it return again in rivers. . . . For all at last return to the sea—to Oceanus, the ocean river, like the ever-flowing stream of time, the beginning and the end.

Carson herself returned to the sea later in the summer of 1951. She went to Bar Harbor, a fashionable summer resort on Mount Desert Island off the Maine coast. Carson went not for the society, but for the seacoast, which she was eager to explore. She then spent August at Woods Hole.

In the fall, though, Carson was forced to exchange the long, lonely stretches of coastline for the crowded city. In October, Carson was scheduled to speak at a book-and-author luncheon in New York. The thought of having to face an audience of 1,500 terrified Carson. She kept her talk brief and informal and included a sound recording of clicking shrimp and other undersea noises.

The following months brought a series of important awards and honors. Carson received the John Burroughs Medal, awarded every year for an outstanding book in natural history. John Burroughs was a very popular American author of the late nineteenth and early twentieth century, who wrote a series of books on birds, flowers, and rural scenes. The New York Zoological Society and the Philadelphia Geographical Society also presented Carson with gold medals.

Her fourth gold medal came from the publishing industry itself. Carson won the National Book Award for the best nonfiction book of 1951. The National Book Awards are annual prizes given for distinguished books written or translated by U.S. citizens. In her acceptance speech, the ever modest author said, "If there is poetry in my book about the sea, it is not because I deliberately put it there, but because no one could write truthfully about the sea and leave out the poetry."

Two honorary degrees recognized Carson's achievement as both a gifted writer and a scientist. Honorary degrees are conferred on people who have distinguished themselves in some way. The people who receive such degrees have not pursued the course of study that would ordinarily lead to a degree. Chatham College awarded Carson a doctor of literature degree; Oberlin College, a doctor of science degree. These degrees are the highest ones that can be awarded in their respective fields.

The huge success of *The Sea Around Us* made Oxford University Press decide to bring out a new edition of *Under the Sea Wind*. This all-but-forgotten book quickly joined *The Sea Around Us* on the nonfiction best-seller list.

Then one of Carson's wildest dreams came true. The RKO film company bought the motion picture rights to *The Sea Around Us*. Unfortunately, when Carson saw the film and read the script, which had been written in the studio, she was extremely disappointed. Despite her dislike of the film, it went on to win an Oscar for the best full-length documentary film in 1953.

Otherwise, all the recognition she received pleased Carson. Her only regret was that the various public appearances she was obliged to make took valuable time away from the planning and writing of her next book.

8

To the Beach with a Bucket

Rachel Carson's next book started with a Sunday morning stroll on the outer beaches of Cape Cod. The strollers were guests of Rosalind Wilson, an editor at the Houghton Mifflin Company. They found the beach strewn with horseshoe crabs. Thinking that the crabs had been stranded by the previous night's storm, the guests carefully returned them to the sea. Rosalind Wilson was horrified when she found out what they had done. By returning the crabs to the sea, her guests had unwittingly interrupted the mating process of the horseshoe crabs.

Back at her office on Monday, Wilson dashed off a note to another editor, Paul Brooks. She wanted him to find an author for a guide to seashore life. With such a guide in hand, people would be less likely to make mistakes like that of the past weekend. Not long afterward, Carson met with the editors at Houghton Mifflin about another project. They proposed that she do the guide, and she accepted.

Carson was excited about the project. She felt that the new book would serve as a companion to *The Sea Around Us*. In that book, she had dealt with the physical life of the ocean. Now she would be dealing with the biological life of one part of the sea. The shore appealed to Carson for two reasons. First, almost anyone could visit it. Second, the shore was a transition area between land and sea. In order to survive, the shore creatures had to be able to adapt to the conditions of both land and sea.

Carson knew that the project would involve many field trips to places along the coast. She felt she couldn't do all this work while continuing with her job at the Fish and Wildlife Service. She applied for a year-long leave of absence without pay. This would give her the time she needed, but what about money?

In the fall of 1950, *The Sea Around Us* had yet to be published. Carson had no idea the book would make her rich as well as famous. She applied to the John S. Guggenheim Foundation for funds to support her work. The foundation came through with a grant of $4,000 the following spring. Carson later returned this money when *The Sea Around Us* became a best-seller. She could now afford to resign from the Fish and Wildlife Service and realize her old dream of living by her writing alone.

It was probably just as well that Carson left the service when she did. The 1950s were not a good time for conservation-minded people in government. The new president, Dwight D. Eisenhower, appointed an Oregon automobile dealer, Douglas McKay, to be secretary of the interior. McKay called conservationists "long-haired punks." He fired Albert M. Day, the highly respected head of the Fish and Wildlife Service. McKay allowed private companies to remove oil and minerals from wildlife refuges and other land managed by the service.

Carson protested the firing of Day in a letter to the *Washington Post*. She warned that "the way is being cleared for a raid upon our natural resources that is without parallel within the present century."

Carson's resignation went into effect in June 1952. She spent the spring and part of the summer exploring the coastline around Charleston, South Carolina, and that of the Florida Keys. The Florida Keys are a chain of small coral and limestone islands and reefs—ridges at or near the surface of the water—that form the southern tip of Florida. They contain the only coral reefs within the United States. Another unique feature of the Keys is their mangrove forests. Mangroves are tropical trees with branches that spread and send down roots, forming more trunks. The trees grow right out into the water, creating swamps and eventually islands.

This very different kind of coastline fascinated Carson. A stranger who was waiting in the Keys for the same bus as Carson told her she looked as though she were going out to discover a new world.

Carson's companion on many of her field trips was her co-worker and good friend from the Fish and Wildlife Service, artist Bob Hines. At her suggestion, Houghton Mifflin hired Hines to do the illustrations for the guide.

Carson and Hines agreed that most of the drawings should be made from live specimens collected on location. When the tide was out, Carson spent hours collecting specimens. She and Hines brought them back in a bucket, and Hines made his drawings. When he was finished, Carson put the specimens back into the bucket and returned them to their natural places along the shore.

Once when Carson was wading in the waters off one of

the Florida Keys, she came across a kind of starfish she had never seen before. It was so lovely that she had no wish to "collect" it. Instead, she stood beside the starfish for a long time, "lost to all but its extraordinary and fragile beauty."

On other occasions, Carson rescued creatures that the waves had washed onto the beach. She helped an octopus "in distress" out beyond the breakers. She also waded into chilly March water along the South Carolina coast to return a jellyfish to the sea.

Sometimes Carson herself needed rescuing. In the Florida Keys, Bob Hines had to carry her out of a mangrove swamp. She had stayed until she was so tired she could barely move. Later, Hines lifted Carson out of barnacle-covered tide pools at Boothbay Harbor, Maine. Although she was chilled to the bone, Carson wouldn't leave by herself.

Hines was good company, too. When he couldn't remember the scientific name of the creature he was draw-ing, Hines would call it a "wee beast." This and other remarks of his often brought forth a tingling laugh from Carson.

In 1953 the success of *The Sea Around Us* made it possible for Carson to realize another long-cherished dream. She bought a tract of land in West Southport, Maine, overlooking Sheepscot Bay. Here she built a one-story cottage on the rocks. Only a few steps separated the window with a view of the setting sun from the dark line of high tide.

Two new friends in Maine also shared with Carson the excitement of working on the book. Carson's neighbors were a Massachusetts couple, Dorothy and Stanley Freeman. The Freemans had read *The Sea Around Us* and enjoyed it tremendously. Learning that its author was building a house close to their summer cottage, the Freemans sent Carson a friendly, welcoming note. Carson was delighted by the note.

She wrote back that she would like to call on the Freemans the following summer.

Unfortunately, the illness of Carson's mother kept them from moving to the cottage until July. Then, immediately after their arrival, a beloved cat died of pneumonia. Both Carson and her mother were deeply saddened by the loss. Maria Carson suffered a relapse as a result.

When Carson was able to call on the Freemans, she found they shared her love of nature. Dorothy Freeman had worked for the Agricultural Extension Service of the Department of Agriculture. She had also served as the leader of a 4-H Club for girls. Stanley studied agricultural problems for a Massachusetts feed company. He was also an amateur photographer and small-boat sailor. Carson and the Freemans quickly became close friends.

Dorothy Freeman knew this part of the Maine coast like the back of her hand. She took Carson to see one of her favorite spots—a tide pool in a cave whose entrance was above water only during the year's lowest tides. The entrance was too small for a person to enter. But Carson was able to peek in. She glimpsed a tiny starfish hanging by a single tube foot from the roof of the cave. The starfish was reaching down to touch its own reflection in the pool below.

For someone writing a book about the seashore, the rugged Maine coast turned out to be the ideal location. Carson rose early in the morning to take advantage of low tide. She often followed a path through an evergreen forest to reach the shore. Even in the woods, she could smell the salt of the sea, hear the "whispered echo" of the surf, and feel the softness of the fog. Coming upon the shore this way gave her the sense of a world being newly created.

When the tide raced in again, Carson returned to the cottage with the creatures she had collected. She spent hours

83

studying them under a magnifying glass or under the lenses of her powerful new binocular microscope. Carson had always wanted such a microscope. But only after the success of *The Sea Around Us* was she able to afford one.

Low tide didn't come again until after dark. So, flashlight in hand, Carson made her way across the slippery rocks with the specimens she was returning. Everywhere she looked, she could see crabs scuttling about. The crabs with their strange, shadowy shapes changed what had been a familiar place into a "goblin world."

Sometimes Carson and her mother took short car trips along the Maine coast. While Rachel explored the beaches,

Rachel Carson explores a tide pool near her summer house at West Southport on the Maine coast.

Maria Carson stayed in the car, writing letters. Maria Carson was enormously proud of her daughter's success. To passersby who stopped to chat, she would say, "That's my daughter, Rachel Carson. She wrote *The Sea Around Us*."

Carson and her mother also enjoyed beach picnics with Bob Hines and the Freemans. Carson even went sailing with the Freemans in their sixteen-foot sloop, although small boats made her nervous. On clear summer nights, Carson and the Freemans often sat on the veranda of the Freemans' house. They watched the moon travel across the water until it reached a large tide pool. When the moon was reflected in the pool, they applauded.

By this time, Carson's two nieces were grown up and married. But Marjie, whom Carson was especially close to, brought her infant son, Roger, to visit. Together aunt and niece found a ten-inch starfish, and photographed Roger holding it.

Fall came all too soon. The Freemans left for their home in Massachusetts. Since Carson's house was designed for summer use only, the water supply had to be turned off when it got too cold. Otherwise, the pipes would freeze in the winter. Nevertheless, Carson and her mother stayed until the last possible moment. In October, they watched the autumn colors turn vivid and the trees fill with birds migrating south for the winter. There were so many birds that Rachel and Maria often ate their breakfast with binoculars in hand. Finally, late in the month, Carson and her mother reluctantly returned to Silver Spring.

Carson was back in Maine as early as possible the next summer and the summer after that. Published in the fall of 1955, *The Edge of the Sea* reflected the joy of discovery Carson had felt in Maine and other places along the shore. More than her two other books, Carson had "lived" this one. She

85

dedicated the book "To Dorothy and Stanley Freeman, who have gone down with me into the low-tide world and have felt its beauty and mystery."

The Edge of the Sea was different from Carson's two previous books in terms of both content and form. While Carson used storytelling in *Under the Sea Wind*, in *The Sea Around Us* she presented the facts in a straightforward, but extremely vivid manner. In *The Edge of the Sea*, on the other hand, Carson's approach most closely resembled that of the essay. The author of an essay examines a particular subject from his or her own personal viewpoint.

The book begins with a series of recollections of places along the coast that had stirred Carson deeply. One such place was the sea cave Dorothy Freeman had shown Carson. Carson also recalled "a twilight hour on a great beach on the coast of Georgia":

> I had come down after sunset and walked far out over sands that lay wet and gleaming, to the very edge of the retreating sea. . . . The only sounds were those of the wind and the sea and the birds. . . .
>
> The flats took on a mysterious quality as dusk approached and the last evening light was reflected from scattered pools and creeks. Then birds became only dark shadows with no color discernible. Sanderlings scurried across the beach like little ghosts.

The rest of the book combines Carson's personal experiences of exploring the Atlantic coast with factual information about the plants and animals of the shore. *The Edge of the Sea* ends as it began, with Carson in Maine. As she sits in her study at night, watching the fog roll in and hearing the sound of the rising tide, she thinks of how the tide is also rising on other shores. Then, in her thoughts, these very different shores "are made one by the unifying touch of the sea."

Carson's viewpoint in *The Edge of the Sea* is both personal and ecological—that is, she is concerned with the relationship of the shore creatures to each other and to their environment. As she writes in the preface, or introductory remarks, "To understand the life of the shore, it is not enough to pick up an empty shell and say 'This is a murex,' or 'That is an angel wing.'" Instead, Carson wants her readers to understand the whole life of the creature that lived in the shell: "how it survived amid surf and storms, what were its enemies, how it found food and reproduced its kind, what were its relations to the particular sea world in which it lived."

Carson divides the seashores of the world into three basic types: the rocky shores, the sand beaches, and the coral reefs. She shows how each has its typical community of plants and animals. Since the Atlantic coast of the United States is one of the few places in the world that provide examples of each type of seashore, she uses it for her "pictures of shore life."

In her studies of the shore, two things made an especially strong impression on Carson. One was the blind will of the shore creatures to survive. The other was the enormous power of the sea itself. According to Carson, human beings are "uneasy trespassers" in the sea-swept world of the shore.

When the first installment of *The Edge of the Sea* appeared in *The New Yorker,* Carson's long-time admirer Edwin Way Teale wrote: "You have done it again!" Reviewers and readers agreed wholeheartedly with Teale. *The Edge of the Sea* leaped onto the *New York Times* best-seller list and stayed there for twenty-three weeks. The National Council of Women of the United States cited the book as "the outstanding book of the year." Carson also won the Achievement Award of the American Association of University Women.

Countless readers wrote Carson, telling her how much they loved her new book. Carson took her fan mail seriously and tried to answer as many letters as she could. Sometimes the letters led to new friendships. For example, a blind girl wrote to say she had greatly enjoyed *The Edge of the Sea* after hearing it read as a talking book, a recording of a book made for the blind. The blind girl hoped to become a writer herself. Carson wrote back an encouraging letter, and a long correspondence followed.

A less ambitious author might have taken a rest at this point. But as Carson put it, "No writer can stand still." Although she wasn't ready to start another major book project just yet, she busied herself with two smaller projects.

The first was a television program, sponsored by *Omnibus* magazine, on the subject of clouds. Dr. Vincent Schaeffer, a leading meteorologist and expert on clouds and cloud photography, was making the film. A meteorologist is a scientist who studies the weather.

Carson's task was to write the script that would go with the film. She had never done anything for television before. But since millions of Americans owned sets by the mid-1950s, television was a way to reach a huge audience. Also, clouds had long fascinated Carson. At one point, she had even considered writing a book called *The Air Around Us*.

Something About the Sky was broadcast on March 11, 1956.

In the script she wrote, Carson showed that she could write as vividly about "the ocean of air" as "the ocean of water." The second project was even closer to Carson's heart. It was an article for the *Woman's Home Companion* about encouraging children to appreciate nature. Titled "Help Your Child to Wonder," the article drew upon Carson's experiences with her grandnephew Roger. Every summer from the time he was an infant, Roger had visited Carson in Maine. The article opens with a description of how Carson introduced him to the ocean:

> One stormy autumn night when my nephew Roger was about twenty months old I wrapped him in a blanket and carried him down to the beach in the rainy darkness. Out there, just at the edge of where-we-couldn't see, big waves were thundering in, dimly seen white shapes that boomed and shouted and threw great handfuls of froth at us. Together we laughed for pure joy—he a baby meeting for the first time the wild tumult of Oceanus, I with the salt of half a lifetime of sea love in me. But I think we felt the same spine-tingling response to the vast, roaring ocean and the wild night around us.

Carson believed that "a child's world is fresh and new and beautiful, full of wonder and excitement." Unfortunately, many children lose this sense of wonder by the time they become adults. If a child is to keep alive this sense of wonder, he or she needs the companionship of at least one adult to share it with him or her. Carson realized, however, that many parents feel they aren't up to this task because they lack specific knowledge of the natural world. To these, she said, "It is not half so important to *know* as to *feel*."

Why keep alive a sense of wonder? Near the end of the article, Carson answered her own question this way: "Those who dwell, as scientists or laymen, among the beauties of nature and mysteries of the earth are never alone or weary of life. Whatever the vexations or concerns of their personal lives, their thoughts can find paths that lead to inner contentment and to renewed excitement in living. Those who contemplate the beauty of the earth find reserves of strength that will endure as long as life lasts."

Carson believed that people can gain much from simply visiting places of great natural beauty. She felt it was important that such places be preserved. Now that she was a successful writer, she hoped to use some of the money earned from her books to this end.

One place Carson particularly wanted to save was a rugged strip of Maine coastline. Her idea was to put together a huge anthology, or collection, of nature writing. She would use the money made from the sales of the anthology to purchase this strip of coastline and preserve it for all time.

Nothing ever came of this idea, because the land turned out to be much too expensive. Also, another family tragedy occurred in the winter of 1957. Carson's niece Marjorie had long suffered from poor health. That February she died of pneumonia. Since Marjorie's husband had died when their son, Roger, was a baby, her death left him an orphan. Carson felt that in their small family she was the logical one to care for Roger Christie. So when she was nearly fifty she became the adoptive mother of a five-year-old.

Caring for both Roger and her ailing, eighty-eight-year-old mother took up a great deal of Carson's time. In addition, she had to supervise the building of a new house in Silver Spring. Carson decided to build a house when she couldn't find one to buy that met her new requirements. The new home was a big brick house, located on a large wooded lot about twenty miles from downtown Washington.

With so much to do, Carson had to give up her writing for a while. Before the end of the year, however, she accepted an assignment from *Holiday* magazine to write an article about the seashore. The article was to appear in a special issue of the magazine devoted to "Nature's America." Carson considered expanding the article into a small book. The book would be aimed at saving those parts of the shoreline that were still unspoiled.

Then in January 1958, Carson received a letter that drastically changed her plans. This letter spurred her to write a very different kind of book—one that would be both more important and more controversial than anything else she had ever written.

CHAPTER

9

Silent Spring, Noisy Summer

"The mosquito control plane flew over our small town last summer," Olga Owens Huckins wrote to her friend Rachel Carson in January 1958. Huckins and her husband had a small private bird sanctuary in Duxbury, Massachusetts. "Since we live close to the marshes we were treated to several lethal [deadly] doses [of poison]." Huckins went on to describe the horrible consequences:

> The "harmless" shower bath killed seven of our lovely songbirds outright. We picked up three dead bodies the next morning right by the door. They were birds that had lived close to us, trusted us, and built their nests in our trees year after year. The next day three were scattered around the bird bath. (I had emptied it and scrubbed it after the spraying but YOU CAN NEVER KILL DDT.) On the following day one robin

dropped suddenly from a branch in our woods. We were too heartsick to hunt for other corpses. All these birds died horribly, and in the same way. Their bills were gaping open, and their splayed [spread out] claws were drawn up to their breasts in agony....

Air spraying where it is not needed or wanted is inhuman, undemocratic, and probably unconstitutional. For those of us who stand helplessly on the tortured earth, it is intolerable.

Huckins begged Carson to find someone in Washington who could help. In the end, Carson's search for that "someone" led back to herself.

The poison that killed Olga Huckins's robins was a fairly new discovery. In 1939, a Swiss chemist, Paul Müller, developed DDT (dichloro-diphenyl-trichloro-ethane). (Earlier, in 1874, a German graduate student had also developed DDT. But he couldn't find a use for it, so he did not try to market it.) Geigy, the chemical company where Müller worked, wanted him to find a substance to mothproof woolen clothing.

Müller discovered that DDT was a much more persistent poison than older pesticides. Pesticides are poisons that kill insects considered nuisances. The powder went on killing flies Müller placed in a glass box with it for days after the first application. It remained deadly even after Müller had several times scrubbed the box with soap and water.

Swiss farmers started using DDT to keep insects from destroying their crops. During World War II, the United States used the new poison to prevent a deadly outbreak of typhus in Italy. Body lice carry the disease. Used as a dusting powder, DDT killed the lice.

Government officials and scientists hailed DDT as a

Across the United States, thousands of pounds of pesticides were used to protect farm crops from insects. This plane was dusting a cotton crop to protect it from grasshoppers. In the late 1950s, Rachel Carson began to research the possible dangers of pesticides.

chemical miracle. In 1948, Paul Müller won a Nobel Prize in medicine and physiology for his discovery. Each year, Nobel Prizes are awarded to people in different fields whose work makes a valuable contribution to humanity.

After World War II, U.S. chemical companies like Shell and Monsanto began manufacturing DDT in large quantities. They also developed more than 200 other chemical pesticides. Farmers, foresters, and home gardeners were delighted. Every year, they bought as much as half a billion pounds of DDT and related poisons for use in their battle against bugs. The U.S. Department of Agriculture launched huge spraying programs to wipe out specific pests. The U.S. Public Health Service also used pesticides to destroy disease-carrying insects.

However, some biologists, wildlife specialists, and medical experts were becoming alarmed. They worried about the effects of long-lasting poisons like DDT on the environment. In 1946, Elmer Higgins and Clarence Cottam of the Fish and Wildlife Service wrote scientific papers about DDT. They warned about the danger it posed to fish and wildlife. A year earlier, Carson herself had suggested a similar article to *Reader's Digest*. But the magazine wasn't interested in printing anything negative about DDT.

Now, thirteen years later, in 1958, Olga Huckins's letter jolted Carson back to the subject of DDT. She made phone calls, wrote letters, and tracked down facts. The more she learned, the more angry and disturbed she became. Once again, Carson suggested an article to *Reader's Digest*. But neither it nor the various other popular magazines she tried were ready to criticize DDT.

Carson then considered writing a short book about the subject. She doubted, and so did many of her friends, that such a book would be a best-seller. One reason that *The Sea Around Us* was so popular was that it took readers away from the stresses and strains of everyday life. A book on the dangers of pesticides would offer no such comforting escape, Carson knew. But she felt she had to write it anyway. "There would be no peace for me if I kept silent," she said.

In May 1958, Carson signed a contract for a book with the working title of *The Control of Nature* with Houghton Mifflin, the publisher of *The Edge of the Sea*. She hoped to have a complete manuscript by early July, for publication in

A cowbird killed by pesticide applied to a corn field.

January 1959. Carson little dreamed that work on the book would take up the next four years of her life.

But the project kept growing. One piece of information led to another. New areas of research opened up almost every day. Carson corresponded with experts all over the world. Her reputation as the author of *The Sea Around Us* helped open many doors.

Dr. C. J. Briejèr, of the Plant Protection Service in the Netherlands, proved particularly helpful. So did Dr. Clarence Cottam. Cottam had been assistant director of the Fish and Wildlife Service when Carson was editor-in-chief of publications. He was now director of the Welder Wildlife Foundation in Sinton, Texas. Cottam provided Carson with details about the disastrous failure of one of the U.S. Department of Agriculture's mass spraying programs.

This was an effort to get rid of the fire ant in the Southwest. Not only did the spraying fail to wipe out the fire ant, but it killed off huge numbers of livestock and wildlife.

The vast amount of research involved wasn't the only thing that kept Carson from finishing the book on schedule. Family responsibilities also took up her time. Carson now had a devoted housekeeper, Ida Sprow, to prepare meals and cope with domestic chores on weekdays from nine to four. But these tasks fell to Carson herself evenings and weekends.

Carson also looked after Roger, who entered the first grade in 1958, and her ailing, almost ninety-year-old mother. In December 1958 Maria Carson died. Weeks passed before her grieving daughter was able to get back to work on the book.

Carson now hoped to complete the manuscript by fall 1959, for publication early in 1960. But that summer health problems got in the way. Carson had trouble with her sinuses—small passages in the human skull. Also, Roger developed an infection that kept him out of summer camp and at home.

In addition, Carson had to devote some of her time to a revision of *The Sea Around Us*. Since the book's publication, oceanographers had made a number of new discoveries. Carson's publisher wanted her to update the book. Some of Carson's own ideas about the oceans had also changed. She was no longer so optimistic that the sea would be safe from tampering by human beings.

During World War II, scientists in the United States had developed a powerful new weapon, the atomic bomb. Throughout the 1950s, testing of this new weapon continued. Scientists also tried to find peacetime uses for atomic power. The testing and experiments produced dangerous radioactive wastes that had to be disposed of somehow.

The Atomic Energy Commission decided to sink containers of the waste deep in the ocean. However, tests later showed that these sealed barrels could be smashed by the pressure of the ocean and their contents released. In the preface to the 1961 edition of *The Sea Around Us*, Carson warned about the pollution of the oceans by radioactive wastes:

It is a curious situation that the sea, from which all life first arose, should now be threatened by the activities of one form of that life. But the sea, though changed in a sinister way, will continue to exist; the threat is rather to life itself.

Meanwhile, the public was waking up to the dangers of pesticides and other chemicals. Just before Thanksgiving Day 1959, the U.S. Food and Drug Administration ordered that cranberries sprayed with a powerful weed killer, aminotriazole, be withdrawn from the market. Tests had shown that even low doses of this weed killer could cause cancer in rats. Then came the thalidomide tragedies. Mothers who had taken this drug while they were pregnant gave birth to severely deformed children.

Carson realized that disturbing events like these would serve to create an audience for her book—if she could just finish it. To assist with correspondence and other paperwork, she hired a secretary and general helper, Mrs. Jeanne Davis. With experience on several scientific journals, Davis was an able assistant and also became a good friend.

Thanks to Davis's help, Carson was getting more done. But she felt run-down a lot of the time. In spring 1960, she went to a Washington doctor for a check-up. The doctor discovered a cancerous growth on one of Carson's breasts and operated to remove it.

The following fall, Carson learned that despite the operation, the cancer had spread. She went to a specialist and began a series of radiation treatments. The treatments greatly weakened her. But in the intervals between them, Carson continued to work on the book. The encouragement of friends and her own strong belief that she had a crucial message to deliver kept her going.

That winter Carson developed a bacterial infection that settled in her knees and ankles. The infection made it almost impossible for her to walk. Confined to her bed, she nevertheless took great pleasure in the first signs of spring. One March morning, she was awakened by the cries of geese. She managed to stagger to the window, calling to Roger to share the excitement. The day before, Carson had heard the first robin song of the year.

Even as she rejoiced in the robin's clear-throated song, Carson knew that the day might come when there would be

During 1961, Rachel Carson worked on the manuscript for her new book, Silent Spring.

no more birds left to sing. She had written a highly dramatic chapter about the threatened destruction of all bird life by DDT and other chemical poisons. Her editor, Paul Brooks, suggested she call the chapter "Silent Spring." This became the title of the entire book.

Early in 1962, Carson finally completed the manuscript of *Silent Spring*. She sent it off to Paul Brooks at Houghton Mifflin and to William Shawn, the editor of *The New Yorker*. The magazine planned to publish a shortened version of the book in several parts. As soon as he had finished reading the manuscript, Shawn telephoned Carson to tell her how impressed he was.

That night, after Roger was asleep, Carson took her cat Jeffie into the study and played a favorite record of violin music by the German composer Ludwig van Beethoven. For the first time in four years, she felt she could let go and cry with sheer relief.

The previous summer, Carson had told Dorothy Freeman that she could never again listen happily to a thrush song if she had not done all she could to stop the killing of birds by pesticides. Now she had. The book was completed. Its printed words would reach people all over the country and finally the globe. The world would never be the same again.

Why did *Silent Spring* have such a huge impact? The book opens with a chilling picture. Carson describes an imaginary town in the heart of America that lies in the midst of prosperous farms and much natural beauty. The area boasts lovely trees and wildflowers, abundant wildlife and birds. But when a white powder falls from the sky, things start to go wrong. Livestock sicken and die. People become mysteriously ill. There is a strange stillness in the air because the birds have vanished.

What has happened? "No witchcraft, no enemy action had silenced the rebirth of new life in this stricken world," Carson writes. "The people had done it themselves."

What follows is a carefully argued case against the pollution of the planet by chemical pesticides. As in her previous books, Carson's viewpoint is ecological. She says that life on earth is the story of the interaction of living things and their surroundings. Lately, however, human beings have gained great power to change the nature of the world. They can destroy it outright through nuclear war. Or they can poison the world with harmful substances.

Carson doesn't deny that some insects pose threats to human beings. Nor does she deny the need to control insects that carry disease or destroy crops. But she doesn't want people to ruin the environment and themselves in the process.

Carson feels that this is exactly what will happen, however, if people remain ignorant of the nature of the chemical poisons that are being used. "If we are going to live so intimately with these chemicals—eating and drinking them, taking them into the very marrow of our bones—we had better know something about their nature and their power." Carson goes on to provide histories, descriptions, and effects of the various pesticides and herbicides—weed killers—in order of their increasing deadliness.

In separate chapters, Carson shows how these chemicals pollute the water system and soil. She shows how they damage plants and wildlife and kill large numbers of birds and fish. These creatures all die in a horrible manner like Olga Huckins's robins. "By acquiescing in an act that can cause such suffering to a living creature, who among us is not diminished as a human being?" Carson asks.

Carson protests against the "rain of poison" that has

descended on the earth. Government spraying programs were responsible for this poisonous rain. For example, in 1957 the U.S. Department of Agriculture started a campaign to wipe out the gypsy moth. The insect was damaging oaks and other hardwood trees in the Northeast. The gypsy moth normally lives in forests. Nevertheless, the government included a heavily populated area of Long Island, New York, in the program. The planes

> sprayed the quarter-acre lots of suburbia, drenching a housewife making a desperate effort to cover her garden before the roaring plane reached her, and showering insecticide over children at play and commuters at railway stations. At Setauket a fine quarter horse drank from a trough in a field which the planes had sprayed; ten hours later it was dead. Automobiles were spotted with the oily mixture; flowers and shrubs were ruined. Birds, fish, crabs, and useful insects were killed.

A group of concerned citizens had tried to get a court order to stop the spraying. Leading the group was Robert Cushman Murphy, the same well-known scientist who had helped Carson with *The Sea Around Us*. The group failed and had to suffer the consequences. They then fought to get a court order against all future spraying. They took their case all the way to the U.S. Supreme Court. The Court refused to hear the case.

But the resulting publicity made people aware of the enormous power of government pest control programs. It showed them how these programs often violated the rights of private citizens. And all for nothing. The spraying didn't get rid of the gypsy moth.

Government spraying programs aren't the only way in which chemical poisons enter the environment. Anyone, writes Carson, "may walk into a store and, without questions being asked, buy substances of far greater death-dealing power than the medicinal drug for which he may be required to sign a 'poison book' in the pharmacy next door."

In *Silent Spring*, Carson gives numerous examples of human victims of severe chemical poisoning. A baby loses its sight and hearing and suffers frequent muscle spasms after returning to a house sprayed for cockroaches. A tank truck driver becomes seriously ill and dies after sticking his bare hand into a drum containing a powerful chemical poison.

Nevertheless, in *Silent Spring*, Carson is most concerned with the slow, long-term effects of small doses of these chemicals on human beings. Humans take in small amounts of DDT and related poisons with almost every meal they eat. Babies get these poisons in their mother's milk. DDT is stored in blood and body fat, where it tends to build up.

Carson says that she believes that these stored poisons can damage the human liver and nervous system. She also says that she believes that pesticides may change human cells. In this way, the poisons may interfere with the basic processes of life itself.

Carson then tackles the subject of chemical poisons and cancer. She blames the increase in cancer deaths, particularly among American schoolchildren, on DDT and other pesticides. According to Carson, scientists and doctors shouldn't simply seek a cure for cancer. They ought to try to prevent the disease in the first place. They can do so by eliminating as many of these cancer-causing chemicals as possible.

This part of the book turned out to be the most controversial. Critics charged that Carson seized upon cancer because she was suffering from the disease herself.

In fact, Carson did overstate the case here. She could not prove a definite link between human cancer deaths and chemical pesticides. When she wrote *Silent Spring*, such evidence did not exist.

Twenty-odd years later, a 1989 study found no significant link between DDT and the risk of human death by cancer. The scientists who made the study did point out, however, that the study wasn't large enough to detect a small increase in cancer deaths. The National Cancer Institute and the Olin Corporation financed the study. The Olin Corporation had manufactured DDT. If it hadn't been for Carson, the company would probably have never financed the study.

In *Silent Spring*, Carson argues that we can afford to cut down on our use of chemical poisons. Massive spraying kills good insects as well as bad. In this way, it upsets the balance of nature. Some of the good insects prey on the ones considered pests. For example, a single ladybug devours hundreds of aphids and other plant-eating insects. But when we destroy the enemies of pests, we create a situation in which the pests are likely to multiply rapidly.

Also, pests can become resistant to chemical poisons, as Carson shows. This means that in order to kill them, we have to develop even deadlier poisons. Even then we can't be sure that the pests won't become resistant to the new poisons.

In the concluding chapter of *Silent Spring*, Carson proposes an alternative to filling the world with poisonous chemicals. She says that she believes that insect pests can be more effectively controlled with a great deal less damage to the environment by natural or biological means. We can make use of the natural enemies of various pests. We can also introduce diseases that kill specific insects without harming other living things.

Instead of spending millions of dollars to develop stronger poisons, Carson says that she believes that we ought to use the money to finance studies of biological controls. The choice is ours: to preserve or to destroy the earth.

Carson's aim in *Silent Spring* was to persuade as well as to inform readers. So she didn't hesitate to appeal to their emotions. At the same time, however, she was careful to back up broad statements with specific examples. Carson knew that her book would be controversial. She provided fifty-three pages of notes documenting her sources. Throughout the text, she also mentioned specific authorities by name.

Silent Spring contains much that is shocking and horrible. Nevertheless, Carson says that she hopes that "ugly facts" won't dominate the book: "The beauty of the living world I was trying to save has always been uppermost in my mind."

Silent Spring first appeared in *The New Yorker* in June 1962. Right away, it caused a huge sensation. The chemical industry, which made $300 million a year from the sale of DDT and other pesticides, was furious. Velsicol, a chemical company based in Chicago, claimed that the book contained false statements about two of its products, chlordane and heptachlor. It tried to stop publication of the book by Houghton Mifflin with a threatened lawsuit. But when the publisher held its ground, the company backed off.

Having failed to stop publication, the chemical industry now tried to discredit the book. Most individual companies looked to trade, or industry, groups like the National Agricultural Chemicals Association to do this. The organization immediately set aside a quarter of a million dollars "to improve the image of the industry." It put together a publication called *Fact and Fancy*. The publication quoted statements from *Silent Spring*, then supplied "facts" that supposedly disproved the statements.

One company, Monsanto, made fun of the book with a parody called *The Desolate Year*. The parody pictured a world without pesticides in which insects ate up everything in sight. Monsanto sent copies of *The Desolate Year* to newspaper editors and book reviewers all over the country.

Some of the fiercest attacks came from farming magazines and universities involved in farming research. The chemical industry paid for much of this research. For example, a scientist at Michigan State University called Carson's book "more poisonous than the pesticides she condemns."

Another organization that leaped into the attack was the Nutrition Foundation of New York City. Nutrition is the science of how living creatures take in and use food material. Fifty-four companies in the food, chemical, and related industries belonged to the Nutrition Foundation. The foundation gave out money, in the form of research grants, from these companies to the nutrition departments of many famous universities.

One of these was Vanderbilt University. Dr. William Darby, a nutritionist at the university's school of medicine, wrote a widely circulated article criticizing *Silent Spring*. He said that the book should be ignored. The Nutrition Foundation itself distributed a collection of negative reviews, including Darby's.

The chemical industry even managed to win over the medical profession. Many individual doctors and public health experts supported Carson's findings. Nevertheless, the magazine of the American Medical Association (AMA) referred members to the "fact kits" put out by the chemical industry. The magazine advised doctors to use these kits when answering patients' questions about pesticides!

The chemical industry also sent representatives out to speak with groups directly. Attacking *Silent Spring* became a kind of personal mission for one man. Dr. Robert White-Stevens belonged to the Research and Development Department of the American Cyanamid Company, a manufacturer of pesticides. Before the end of 1962, White-Stevens made a total of twenty-eight speeches all over the country. He praised pesticides and charged that *Silent Spring* was filled with false statements.

The controversy spilled over into the popular press. "'Silent Spring' Is Now Noisy Summer" trumpeted a *New York Times* headline in July 1962. *Time* magazine accused Carson of deliberately trying to frighten readers with her "emotional and inaccurate outburst." *Reader's Digest* decided not to print a shortened version of the book, as planned. Instead, it reprinted the *Time* article criticizing *Silent Spring*.

Other publications rushed to Carson's defense, however. The *New York Times* said that if *Silent Spring* helped arouse public concern about chemical poisons, its author deserved a Nobel Prize as much as the inventor of DDT.

Another supporter was Loren Eiseley, a famous anthropologist at the University of Pennsylvania. Anthropologists are scientists who study human cultures. In the *Saturday Review*, Eiseley hailed Carson for courageously choosing to educate people about "a sad, an unpleasant, an un-beautiful topic, and one of our very own making." Loren Eiseley felt that *Silent Spring* should be read by every American who did not want the book's frightening vision of the future to come true.

Many Americans took Eiseley's advice. *Silent Spring*'s official publication date was September 27, 1962. Advance sales amounted to 40,000 copies. By the end of the year, sales totaled well over a quarter of a million copies. In Washington, Senator William Proxmire of Wisconsin and Representative John V. Lindsay of New York read parts of the book into the *Congressional Record*. This is the official transcript of everything that is said in the Senate and the House of Representatives.

In Washington, too, young President John F. Kennedy read *Silent Spring* with great interest. Elected to office in 1960, Kennedy had promised to lead Americans into what he called a "New Frontier." He had already launched a number of bold new programs to promote economic growth and tackle social problems. Now he turned to the environment.

On August 29, 1962, the president held a news conference. A reporter asked Kennedy if he planned to do something about the growing concern about pesticides. The president said, yes, "particularly, since Miss Carson's book." The next day, the White House announced the formation of a special science advisory committee. The committee would study the use and control of pesticides.

Action occurred on the state level as well. By the end of 1962, state legislators all over the country introduced more than forty bills to regulate the use of pesticides. The revolution set in motion by *Silent Spring* was just beginning.

CHAPTER

10

A Tide of Concern for the Environment That Has Not Ebbed

Rachel Carson saw herself as a writer and biologist, not a crusader. She felt that her book spoke for itself. But as the controversy over *Silent Spring* continued to boil over, she decided to answer her critics. Some tried to dismiss Carson as overly emotional—a "hysterical woman." Carson resented the charge. There was something more than "mere feminine intuition" behind her concern about pesticides, she told the National Council of Women of the United States in October 1962.

In a speech at the Women's National Press Club in Washington in December, Carson also discussed the attacks on her. She noted that critics labeled her "a bird lover—a cat lover—a fish lover—a priestess of nature." They also attacked statements she had never made. "Anyone who has really read the book knows that I criticize the modern chemical method not because it *controls* harmful insects but because it controls them *badly* and *inefficiently* and creates many dangerous side effects in doing so." Finally, Carson pointed out that the university scientists who attacked her often received research grants from the chemical industry.

On the evening of April 3, 1963, millions of viewers saw Carson face her critics on a "CBS Reports" program, "The Silent Spring of Rachel Carson." Carson appeared frail, but her manner was composed and calm. Her chief opponent was Dr. Robert White-Stevens of the American Cyanamid Company. He accused Carson of "gross distortions of the actual facts" in her book. According to White-Stevens, "The real threat to the survival of man is in the shape of hordes of insects that can denude our forests, sweep over our crop lands, ravage our food supply." If people were to follow Carson's advice, he said, these insects would once again take over the earth.

Replied Carson: "It is not my contention that chemical pesticides must never be used. I do contend that we have allowed these chemicals to be used with little or no advance investigation of their effect on soil, water, wildlife, and man himself."

Also appearing on the program were several important federal government officials. They included U.S. Secretary of Agriculture Orville Freeman; Dr. Luther Terry, the U.S. surgeon general; and George Larrick, commissioner of the U.S. Food and Drug Administration. Each began by defending the use of pesticides to protect crops and human health. But all ended by admitting that the dangers Carson warned about were real.

White-Stevens wasn't finished, though. He attacked Carson's claim that the balance of nature was important to human survival. He said that human beings had already disrupted this balance with their numbers, their cities, roads, airports, and very way of life.

Carson replied coolly that the balance of nature couldn't be done away with any more than the laws of gravity could. "This doesn't mean that we must not attempt to tilt the balance of nature in our favor; but when we do make this attempt we must know what we're doing. We must know the consequences."

Even as Carson spoke, President Kennedy's science advisory committee was putting the finishing touches on its report on pesticides. During the eight months that the committee was at work, the president had often asked about its progress and urged that the report be published as soon as possible. Carson herself had met at least once with the committee members.

On May 15, 1963, the report finally came out. It criticized the chemical industry, the U.S. Department of Agriculture, and the U.S. Food and Drug Administration for failing to warn the public about pesticides. The report also recognized the important contribution made by Carson's book. "Until the publication of *Silent Spring* by Rachel Carson, people were generally unaware of the toxicity [poisonous nature] of pesticides. The government should present this information to the public in a way that will make it aware of the dangers while recognizing the value of pesticides."

Naturally, Carson was very pleased with the report. But she said that she hoped the government wouldn't stop there. The next step was to act. On May 16, the day after the report was published, Senator Abraham Ribicoff of Connecticut called the first meeting of a special U.S. Senate subcommittee to order. The committee's task was to study how government agencies could work together to prevent or reduce different kinds of pollution. First on the list were chemical pesticides.

On June 4, Carson testified before the committee. She offered a number of recommendations about pesticide use. Carson felt that the rights of private citizens should be protected in government spraying programs. She also called for laws limiting the sale and use of pesticides. She wanted more studies done on the dangers of pesticides to the environment. Carson ended her testimony with a plea for research on new methods of pest control that either eliminated or reduced the use of pesticides.

Carson found the U.S. Senate subcommittee attentive and sympathetic. Still, she didn't expect the praise Senator Ernest Gruening of Alaska heaped on her. Gruening compared *Silent Spring* to *Uncle Tom's Cabin*, Harriet Beecher Stowe's powerful novel attacking slavery. He said that both books had changed the course of history and that Carson had performed an important service by writing hers.

Two days later, Carson again went to the U.S. Senate. This time she testified in favor of two pesticide control bills. One bill would require the U.S. Department of Agriculture to consult with the U.S. Department of the Interior and state agencies before starting pesticide programs that might hurt fish and wildlife. The other bill would require the labeling of pesticides harmful to fish and wildlife.

Before leaving for her beloved Maine, Carson made a final public appearance to accept an important award. Earlier in the year, she had received two other major awards. One was the Schweitzer Medal of the Animal Welfare Institute, an organization devoted to protecting animals. The award was named after Albert Schweitzer, a world-famous humanitarian. Carson had dedicated *Silent Spring* to him. The other was the "Conservationist of the Year" award of the National Wildlife Foundation. The National Wildlife Foundation is a private, nonprofit organization that seeks to protect wildlife and natural resources. Now the National Council of Women in Washington honored Carson with its very first "Woman of Conscience" award.

Late in June, Carson's secretary and assistant, Jeanne Davis, drove her, eleven-year-old Roger, and the cat Jeffie to West Southport, Maine. For once the car didn't contain the manuscript of a book that Carson was working on. Instead, she brought along the huge stack of mail she had received about *Silent Spring*.

Just answering all the letters was a big enough job, especially in Carson's weakened condition. The cancer in her bones made movement difficult, and arthritis crippled her hands. Now, too, Carson suffered from heart trouble. Still, she was able to spend mornings working in her study.

When the weather was fine, she and Dorothy Freeman went on short walks. Carson liked to go to a small clearing in the woods. Here she watched the gulls flying overhead and listened to the songbirds in the trees. She also enjoyed being read to. One of her favorite books was *The Wind in the Willows* by the Scottish author Kenneth Grahame. This delightful children's book tells the story of Rat, Toad, Mole, Badger, and other animals living in the woods, rivers, and fields of England.

Carson still took pleasure in examining tiny sea creatures under her microscope. Only now others had to bring the creatures to her.

As always, the summer passed quickly, and before Carson knew it, it was time to leave. In mid-October, however, she realized a long-cherished dream to see the California redwoods. Although confined to a wheelchair, Carson went with her agent, Marie Rodell, to San Francisco.

Rachel Carson with her best-selling book, Silent Spring, *in 1963.*

She gave a talk at the Kaiser Medical Center. Afterward, Carson and Rodell visited Muir Woods National Monument with a leader of the Sierra Club and his wife. The Sierra Club is a national organization whose goal is the protection of the environment. The conservationist and crusader for national parks John Muir founded the Sierra Club in 1892. The woods themselves take their name from Muir. For Carson, the visit to this spectacular grove of giant redwoods was a great thrill.

In December, Carson went to New York to receive triple honors. She became the first woman to be awarded the medal of the National Audubon Society, its highest award in conservation. Five hundred guests at the ceremony heard Carson describe conservation as "a cause that has no end. There is no point at which we will say 'our work is done.'" A few days later, the American Geographical Society presented Carson with its medal for "distinguished contributions in the fields of conservation and geography."

Most exciting of all was Carson's election to the American Academy of Arts and Letters. Membership in this prestigious organization was limited to fifty and included artists, sculptors, and musicians as well as writers. When Carson became a member, only three other women belonged to the academy. She was thrilled when the academy president, author and critic Lewis Mumford, spoke of her in the same breath as two famous scientists. They were Galileo Galilei, the seventeenth-century Italian astronomer, mathematician, and physicist; and Count Georges Buffon, the eighteenth-century French naturalist.

Earlier, *Life* magazine had reported that Carson was "unmarried but not a feminist [supporter of women's rights]." The magazine quoted her as saying, "I'm not interested in things done by women or by men but in things done by people." Nevertheless, Carson was very much aware of her position as a woman and proud of "firsts" like the Audubon medal and other honors rarely given women.

In the early months of 1964, Carson had periods when she was able to work. Other times, she was in too much pain to do much of anything. She knew her life was drawing to a close. But she still hoped she might be granted another summer in Maine. Carson and Dorothy Freeman talked about plans for the coming summer when Freeman visited early in April. Freeman had come to be with her friend after Marie Rodell had telephoned to say that Carson was declining rapidly.

On April 14, 1964, two days after Freeman's return home, Marie Rodell called to say that Carson had died. She was fifty-six years old.

As Freeman prepared for the sad trip to Washington for the funeral, she came across a note Carson had written her the previous September. Carson and Freeman had spent a beautiful clear fall morning at the tip of the peninsula south of Carson's cottage in Maine. Here they had watched a fall migration of monarch butterflies,

> that unhurried drift of one small winged form after another, each drawn by some invisible force. We talked a little about their life history. Did they return? We thought not; for most, at least, this was the closing journey of their lives.
>
> But it occurred to me this afternoon, remembering, that it had been a happy spectacle, that we had felt no sadness when we spoke of the fact there would be no return. And rightly—for when any living thing has come to the end of its cycle we accept that end as natural. For the Monarch butterfly, that cycle is mea-

sured in a known span of months. For ourselves, the measure is something else, the span of which we cannot know. But the thought is the same: when that intangible cycle has run its course it is a natural and not unhappy thing that a life comes to its end.

On the Sunday following Rachel Carson's death, her friend Dr. Duncan Howlett read this note as part of the service at All Souls Unitarian Church in Washington. He felt it expressed "in a remarkable way the strength, the simplicity, and the serenity that marked her character." Dr. Howlett also hailed Carson as "one of the true prophets of our time."

Rachel Carson was, indeed, a true prophet and pioneer. Thanks to her, the conservation movement not only grew, but took a new direction. In the past, conservationists had been mostly concerned with saving wild areas and wildlife. The "new" conservationists, on the other hand, wanted to save the human race as well. They realized, too, that the problem went beyond pesticides.

Air pollution also posed grave dangers to human health. Smoke from factories and power plants darkened the air over many cities. It combined with exhaust from cars, trucks, and buses to create a smoky fog called smog. Smog irritated people's eyes, throats, and lungs. Some days the smog was so bad in Los Angeles, California, that people were advised not to exercise outdoors.

In addition, smoke from factories and exhaust from vehicles combined with water vapor to form acid rain. This new "rain of poison" destroyed forests and fouled lakes, killing huge numbers of fish.

Water pollution was a serious problem as well. Cities and towns dumped raw sewage into rivers and streams, making them unfit for drinking and unsafe for swimming. Factories also dumped chemicals and other wastes into the water. In 1969, the Cuyahoga River in Cleveland, Ohio, became so polluted with chemicals that it actually caught fire! Accidents to large tankers poured tons of thick, sticky crude oil into the ocean, killing fish, birds, and wildlife and ruining miles of seashore.

Concerned Americans formed groups like Friends of the Earth and Citizens for Clean Air to protest these developments. They became known as environmentalists, because they wanted to protect the whole environment. On April 22, 1970, an estimated 20 million people took part in Earth Day. All over the country, they gathered to call attention to problems of pollution and to discuss ways to improve the environment.

In 1970, the federal government responded to pressure from environmentalists. It created the U.S. Environmental Protection Agency (EPA). The EPA's job was to enforce a whole series of antipollution laws that were passed during the decade. One law prohibited the use of DDT, along with the other long-lasting chemical poisons. Another regulated the use of less dangerous poisons. Still other laws set clean air standards for factories and required automobile manufacturers to put pollution control devices on cars, trucks, and buses. New waste disposal and sewage treatment plants were built to prevent further pollution and clean up rivers and lakes.

During the 1980s, the environmental movement suffered setbacks, however. President Ronald Reagan (1981–1989) and Secretary of the Interior James G. Watt felt that the new laws protecting air and water quality as well as wildlife and wildlife refuges were too stiff. They argued that these laws prevented the kind of industrial development necessary to create jobs and spur the economy. Watt opened government lands to timber and coal companies. He also made over a million acres of seashore available to oil companies for offshore drilling. Environmentalists protested this new raid on the country's natural resources. They forced Watt to resign in 1983.

In 1990, environmentalists scored a major victory when the new president, George Bush, signed a new and tougher clean air law. The new law is designed to greatly reduce both smog and acid rain.

Nevertheless, many difficult problems remain. For example, scientists discovered that the fossil fuels—oil, natural gas, and coal—used to run automobiles and heat homes and businesses release huge amounts of carbon dioxide into the air. The gas forms a kind of blanket, trapping heat in the atmosphere and raising temperatures. Many scientists believe that this so-called greenhouse effect could have serious consequences. The warmer temperatures might cause a partial melting of the polar ice caps. This could raise the level of the sea, flooding many coastal cities. Other parts of the world might suffer severe dry spells.

As environmentalists seek solutions for this and other problems, the shy woman who courageously sounded the initial warning has not been forgotten. Toward the end of her life, Carson had discussed with friends the possibility of forming an organization. This organization would handle requests for information about pesticides and keep up with new developments in the field. After Carson's death, her friends formed such an organization—the Rachel Carson Trust for the Living Environment, now known as the Rachel Carson Council.

While alive, Carson had also been concerned with preserving natural seashore areas. She had willed funds to the Nature Conservancy for this purpose. The Nature Conservancy is an organization that preserves natural areas by purchasing and maintaining them. It owns numerous preserves in many states. Carson also left money to the Sierra Club.

Five years after her death, the federal government set aside a stretch of the Maine coast as the Rachel Carson National Wildlife Refuge. Carson's childhood home in Springdale, Pennsylvania, is now listed on the National Register of Historic Places and houses a museum and ecological center. Carson's picture, like that of other famous Americans, appears on a postage stamp.

In 1980, President Jimmy Carter posthumously (after her death) awarded Carson the highest honor any American not in the armed forces can receive—the Presidential Medal of Freedom. Her adopted son, Roger Christie, accepted the medal on her behalf. As he handed Christie the medal, President Carter paid tribute to Carson's pioneering role:

> Never silent herself in the face of destructive trends, Rachel Carson fed a spring of awareness across America and beyond. A biologist with a gentle, clear voice, she welcomed her audiences to her love of the sea, while with an equally clear determined voice, she warned Americans of the dangers human beings them- selves pose for their own environment. Always con- cerned, always eloquent, she created a tide of environmental consciousness that has not ebbed.

Important Dates

1907 Rachel Carson is born on May 27 in Springdale, Pennsylvania, the daughter of Maria McLean and Robert Warden Carson.

1918 Carson's first published story appears in *St. Nicholas* magazine.

1925 She graduates from Parnassus High School and is awarded a scholarship to attend Pennsylvania College for Women in Pittsburgh.

1929 Carson graduates with highest honors from Pennsylvania College with a degree in biology. After summer study at the Woods Hole Marine Biological Laboratory, she enrolls as a graduate student in zoology at the Johns Hopkins University.

1930–36 She works as a teaching assistant in biology for summer sessions at Johns Hopkins.

1931–33 Carson is a half-time assistant in zoology at the University of Maryland.

1935 Carson's father dies. To support her mother and herself, she gets a job writing radio scripts for the U.S. Bureau of Fisheries.

1936–39 Carson gets a permanent appointment as a junior aquatic biologist at the Bureau of Fisheries. She and her mother move to Silver Spring, Maryland. After the death of her older sister, they take in her two daughters.

1937 "Undersea" is published in *The Atlantic Monthly* and is widely praised.

1941 Carson's first book, *Under the Sea Wind,* is published.

1943–45 Carson writes and edits government booklets encouraging people to eat more fish as a wartime conservation measure.

1947–50 Carson prepares the "Conservation in Action" series for the U.S. Fish and Wildlife Service.

1949 Carson is appointed editor-in-chief for the Fish and Wildlife Service.

1951 *The Sea Around Us* is published and becomes a best-seller.

1952 Carson wins the National Book Award for the best nonfiction book of 1952 and the John Burroughs Medal for a natural history book of outstanding quality. *Under the Sea Wind* is reissued and joins *The Sea Around Us* on the best-seller list. Carson resigns from her government job.

1953 The RKO film *The Sea Around Us* wins an Oscar award for the best full-length documentary of the year. Carson buys land along the Maine coast and builds a cottage there.

1955 Carson's third book, *The Edge of the Sea,* is published and is cited by the National Council of Women of the United States as the "outstanding book of the year."

1956 Carson writes the script for an *Omnibus* TV program on clouds; "Help Your Child to Wonder" appears in the *Woman's Home Companion.*

1957 When her niece Marjorie dies, Carson adopts her five-year-old son, Roger Christie. She builds a new house in Silver Spring.

1958 In January, Carson receives a letter from Olga Huckins that brings her back to the problem of chemical pesticides. In December her mother dies.

1960 Carson has a tumor removed and learns she has cancer.

1962 After three-part condensation in *The New Yorker*, *Silent Spring* is published. The chemical industry attacks Carson personally and scientifically. More than forty bills to regulate the use of pesticides are introduced in state legislatures.

1963 Carson receives the Schweitzer Medal of the Animal Welfare Institute and the "Conservationist of the Year" award from the National Wildlife Federation. On the "CBS Reports" TV show "The Silent Spring of Rachel Carson," she answers her critics. The report of the President's Science Advisory Committee supports Carson's position on pesticides. In December, Carson receives medals from the National Audubon Society and the American Geographical Society. She is also elected to the American Academy of Arts and Letters.

1964 Carson dies on April 14 in Silver Spring, Maryland, of cancer and heart disease.

1970 The Rachel Carson National Wildlife Refuge in Maine is dedicated by the U.S. secretary of the interior.

1980 President Jimmy Carter posthumously awards Carson the Presidential Medal of Freedom, the highest civilian award of the government.

1981 A Rachel Carson stamp is issued by the U.S. Post Office in Springdale, Pennsylvania.

Bibliography

Books

Brooks, Paul. *The House of Life: Rachel Carson at Work.* Boston: Houghton Mifflin, 1972.

————. *Speaking for Nature: How Literary Naturalists from Thoreau to Rachel Carson Have Shaped America.* Boston: Houghton Mifflin, 1980.

Carson, Rachel. *The Edge of the Sea.* Boston: Houghton Mifflin, 1955.

————. *The Sea Around Us,* rev. ed. New York: Oxford University Press, 1961.

————. *The Sense of Wonder.* New York: Harper & Row, 1965.

————. *Silent Spring.* Boston: Houghton Mifflin, 1962.

————. *Under the Sea Wind,* new ed. New York: Oxford University Press, 1952.

Durrell, Lee. *State of the Ark: An Atlas of Conservation in Action.* New York: Doubleday, 1986.

Gartner, Carol B. *Rachel Carson.* New York: Frederick Ungar, 1983.

Graham, Frank, Jr. *Man's Dominion: The Story of Conservation in America.* New York: M. Evans, 1971.

————. *Since Silent Spring.* Boston: Houghton Mifflin, 1970.

Sterling, Philip. *Sea and Earth: The Life of Rachel Carson.* New York: Thomas Y. Crowell, 1970.

Wallace, David Rains. *Life in the Balance.* New York: Harcourt Brace Jovanovich, 1987.

Articles

Carson, Rachel L. "Rachel Carson Answers Her Critics." *Audubon Magazine,* September 1963, pp. 262-5.

————. "Miss Carson Goes to Congress." *American Forests,* October 1963, pp. 20-23.

"For Many a Spring." *Time,* April 24, 1964, p. 73.

"The Gentle Storm Center: A Calm Appraisal of 'Silent Spring'." *Life,* October 12, 1962, pp. 105–106.

"A Life in Nature." *Newsweek,* April 27, 1964, p. 95

"Pesticides: The Price for Progress; Picture in *Silent Spring.*" *Time,* September 28, 1962, p. 45–6.

Udall, Stewart L., "The Legacy of Rachel Carson." *Saturday Review,* May 16, 1964, p. 23.

Index

New Bedford (Massachusetts),
25
New York City, 25, 55, 77
New Yorker, The (magazine), 71,
87, 101, 106
New York Harbor, 25
New York Times, 72, 88, 108
New York Zoological Society,
59, 77
North, Sterling, 8
North Carolina, 45
Norway, 65
Nova Scotia, 67
nutrition, 107
Nutrition Foundation, 107

Oberlin College, 78
ocean and oceanographers,
40–41, 43, 46–51, 58, 62,
63, 64, 65, 66, 67–68, 74–
75, 76, 79, 80, 81, 82, 83,
84, 85–91, 98, 119, 120–
121
octopus, 82
offshore drilling, 120
oil companies, 120
Old Greenwich (Connecticut),
43
Olin Corporation, 104
Omega (college English club),
16
Omnibus (magazine), 88
Oregon, 61
ospreys, 59
The Outermost House (Beston),
69
ovenbird, 19
owls, 2
Oxford University Press, 66,
70, 72, 78

Pacific Ocean, 65
Parnassus High School, 12
passenger pigeons, 49
Peabody High School, 11
Pearl, Raymond, 30
Pearl Harbor (Hawaii), 51
Pelican Island (Florida), 2
Pennsylvania, 1, 2, 3
Pennsylvanian (college
yearbook), 18, 22
Pennsylvania College for
Women (Chatham
College), 13–23, 32, 33
Peru, 65
pesticides, 92–93, 98–99, 101–
102, 104–108, 110–111, 112,
113, 118–119
photographing, 60
physics, 25
pigs, 3, 5, 24
Pinchot, Gifford, 2
Pittsburgh, 3, 11, 13, 18, 30, 32
Plant Protection Service
(Netherlands), 97
pollution, 39, 98, 102, 104–
105, 111, 113, 118–120
Polynesia, 65
porpoises, 48, 64
Porter, Gene Stratton, 7
Portuguese man-of-war, 62
Potter, Beatrix, 7
pronephros, 30, 33
Proxmire, William, 109

rabbits, 3, 5, 76
Rachel Carson Council, 120
radio broadcasts, 37–38
rats, 76
Reader's Digest, 54, 59, 72, 95, 108
Reagan, Ronald, 119

About the Author

Leslie Wheeler is the author of *Jane Addams,* another biography in this series. She has co-authored textbooks in American history and written other biographies. A native of California, Wheeler now divides her time between Cambridge, Massachusetts, and a country home in the Berkshire Hills. When she's not writing, Wheeler enjoys hiking, cross-country skiing, swimming, and observing deer, wild turkeys, and other wildlife near her Berkshire home.